A STEP FURTHER

STEVE ESTES is a graduate of Columbia Bible College and is at present a student at Westminster Theological Seminary. He and his wife Verna are the proud parents of Ryan Glen and Adrienne.

JONI EARECKSON now lives in Southern California where the climate allows her greater mobility and comfort. Through a non-profit organization, Joni and Friends, Joni has begun a new ministry to those who suffer. Information about her artwork is available by writing:

Joni and Friends
P. O. Box 3225
Woodland Hills, CA 91365

A STEP FURTHER

Joni Eareckson Tada & Steve Estes

Illustrated by Joni

ZONDERVAN
PUBLISHING HOUSE

The poem by Marion Donaldson on page 90 is used by permission of the author.

Unless otherwise indicated, Old Testament references are from the New American Standard Bible and the New Testament references are from the New International Version.

Library of Congress Cataloging in Publication Data

Eareckson, Joni.
A step further.
Bibliography: p.
1. Tetraplegia—Biography. 2. Eareckson, Joni.
I. Estes, Steve, joint author. II. Title
RC406.T4E19 362.4'3'0926 [B] 78-12084
ISBN 0-310-23972-9

Cover photo by Dick Mettee

Printed in the United States of America

83 84 85 86 87 88 — 20 19 18 17 16

To Verna
wife, dear friend, and God's servant

THANKS TO

Jay—for being part of the team that put this book together.

Verna—fastest fingers in the east (on a typewriter).

Judy Markham—our editor extraordinaire, the unsung hero of many books, including this one.

Elisabeth Elliot and *Margaret Clarkson*—for what they teach through example.

Dr. Richard Gaffin and Dr. George Schelzel—for their suggestions and encouragement.

The congregation of the *Evangelical Free Church of Hershey, Pa.*—for "loaning out" *Steve.*

Special thanks for *all those friends* who helped pray this book into being.

Contents

A Personal Note to You . . .

Those of you who read my first book, *Joni*, will remember my spiritual journey to accept my handicap and the life God had planned for me in a wheelchair. In writing it, I shared some general ideas about God's hand and purposes in our suffering. I was surprised and pleased to receive thousands of letters from people who could easily identify with my bouts of depression, despair, and loneliness. Many wrote that they had found encouragement and answers for facing their own trials. I never dreamed people could have such a wide spectrum of needs. Letters came from parents with mongoloid babies, lonely widows in nursing homes, husbands facing suicidal despair, housewives on the verge of nervous breakdowns, and teen-agers locked in guilt-ridden love relationships.

At first I was overwhelmed by the thought of writing this second book in response to the needs of so many—especially for those who are puzzled over the "whys" of their own suffering and how to respond to it. Then I was reminded of the many people who had counseled and helped me in my own earlier desperate search and wrestling with God. As many of you know from reading my first book, God used a young man named Steve Estes to help shape my thinking and my faith in a special way. Out of our Timothy and Paul relationship, a real love for God and His Word began growing in me. In the eleven years I have known Steve, God has continued to encourage and teach me through this dear brother. The seeds that were planted in my life through our friendship are still bearing fruit.

Since God used Steve to help me search through my questions and discover answers for myself (the same questions people are asking in their letters), it seemed only appropriate to ask my "Paul" to help me write this book. After much prayer, research, and labor, it is with great excitement and joy that we have finished our task.

These chapters are the result of much study and thought. I think my favorite, and the one that was most fun to write, is "Heaven." It shines with the kind of joy I feel about going there. If I had to choose one chapter as the most important, it would be "Let God Be God." For only when I began to get a proper view of God was I able to come to grips with my wheelchair. The section that was the most difficult to write was "Healing: A Piece of the Puzzle?" It is weightier than the rest, so if you're not grappling with the issue of miraculous healing, feel free to just skim over it. But I must say that I feel its message is tremendously needed today.

This book then is a step further in the sharing of my life with you—a step further into more struggles and lessons, downfalls and victories. I don't pretend to answer all the questions about the puzzle of our pain and suffering on this earth. Instead, it is a personal look at how God has used people and events in my life to reveal more of Himself. It is the story of how I've learned to respond to the trials He brings into my life.

Because of the comfort I have received, I hope God will use my life and this book to encourage and build you up as you respond to your own trials and walk with our Lord. Most of all, it is my prayer that we may all learn more fully to lift up God and give Him the glory as we suffer for His sake.

In Jesus' Love,

Joni

Introduction

> Once again, I desperately wanted to kill myself. Here I was, trapped in this canvas cocoon. I couldn't move anything except my head. Physically, I was little more than a corpse. I had no hope of ever walking again. I could never lead a normal life and marry Dick. *In fact, he might even be walking out of my life forever,* I concluded. I had absolutely no idea of how I could find purpose or meaning in just existing day after day—waking, eating, watching TV, sleeping.
>
> Why on earth should a person be forced to live out such a dreary existence? How I prayed for some accident or miracle to kill me. The mental and spiritual anguish was as unbearable as the physical torture.
>
> But once again, there was no way for me to commit suicide. This frustration was also unbearable. I was despondent, but I was also angry because of my helplessness. How I wished for strength and control enough in my fingers to do something, anything, *to end my life.* (December 1967, from the book *Joni*)

As I sit on our porch balcony overlooking the surrounding hills of our horse farm and take in all the smells and sounds of this pretty summer day, it's hard to believe I ever had thoughts like that. In fact, I almost can't remember what feeling that way was like. Oh, I'm still paralyzed—still can't walk, still need to be bathed and dressed. But I'm no longer depressed. And to be honest, I can even say that I'm actually glad for the things which have happened to me.

Glad? How can that be? What has made the difference? My artwork and my supportive family and friends helped pull me out of my depression. But the heartfelt gratitude I have for this life in a wheelchair could only have come from God and His Word. They helped me piece together some of the puzzle which was so confusing. It took some seeking and studying. But today as I look back, I am convinced that the whole ordeal of my paralysis was inspired by His love. I wasn't a rat in a maze. I wasn't the brunt of some cruel divine joke. God had *reasons* behind my suffering, and learning some of them has made all the difference in the world. He has reasons for your suffering, too.

PUTTING TOGETHER THE PUZZLE OF SUFFERING

1 We're In This Together

When I first began realizing all the adjustments that being paralyzed involves, I thought to myself, *My lot in life is harder than anyone else's. How many people have the humiliation of needing someone else to bathe them? Or empty their leg bag? What other girl can't even scratch her own shoulder or comb her own hair?*

Of course, it wasn't long before I was forced to realize that many, many people face problems just like mine—or worse. Every day thousands of people in hospitals and nursing homes all around the world need to be bathed and have their leg bags emptied. Many victims of paralysis have less movement than I do. Some have lost their limbs altogether or have been grotesquely deformed by disease. Others are terminally ill. To top it off, a good percentage of these folks have families who are either unable or unwilling to care for them at home (if they're fortunate enough to have families at all).

It's a kind of scale, I finally reasoned. *Every person alive fits somewhere onto a scale of suffering that ranges from little to much.*

And it's true. Wherever we happen to be on that scale—that is, however much suffering we have to endure—there are always those below us who suffer less, and those above who suffer more. The problem is we usually like to compare ourselves only with those who suffer less. That way we can pity ourselves and pretend we're at the top of the scale. But when we face reality and stand beside those who suffer more, our purple-heart medals don't shine so brightly.

A mile from the house in Baltimore where I grew up, a beautiful children's hospital lays nestled among several acres of grassy hills and giant elms. Sometimes after school I would ride my bicycle there or kick up leaves during an autumn afternoon walk, enjoying the beauty outside, seldom thinking of the children inside. I never compared myself with them. I only stacked myself up against so-and-so at school who was prettier than I. Caught up in my life as a high school sophomore, it didn't dawn on me that my problems were nothing compared with the problems of kids who had been confined to those buildings for years. Who cared about crippled children? Or suppertime lectures from mom about starving kids in India? I had *important* things to worry about—like dates and friends and field hockey games!

But not long after my accident I underwent several weeks of operations in that very hospital. When God moved *me* a few notches up the scale of suffering—ah, then it was a different story. *Now* the sterile smells and lonely, institutional atmosphere became more than just something I'd seen on a TV medical show. A whole new world had opened up and become real to me, an unpleasant world at that.

I was eventually to come to the conclusion that *one of God's purposes in increasing our trials is to sensitize us to people we never would have been able to relate to otherwise.*

Let me share with you one reason this is so important. I have observed how people who have known deep suffering are sometimes turned off by the glowing testimonies of Christians who have had life easy. Try to imagine yourself as a terminally ill patient watching television from your hospital bed. How do you think you'd respond if an attractive and talented young Christian, with seemingly everything going for him, suddenly appeared on the screen sharing how Christ can give a person victory over all of life's trials? It would be hard to stifle thoughts like: *What does this guy know about life? He can't even imagine what it's like to really hurt. If he had to face the problems I face, he'd drop that Colgate smile and "Jesus gives you joy" routine.*

It would be nice if the Christian message could be accepted or rejected on its merits alone. But the fact is that few of us can ever divorce a product from the person who sells it.

Now I'm not saying the answer is to go out, break your neck, and buy a wheelchair so people will listen to you! Even being paralyzed I've met people who had difficulty listening to me talk about suffering. All they could see was the contrast between my good health and their chronic disease, my traveling opportunities and their confinement, my supportive family and their dead family.

What I am saying is that to reach and comfort someone, it sometimes takes a person with a similar problem. No one person can reach everyone. I can empathize with quadriplegics. You, perhaps cannot. But you can identify with difficulties I have not experienced . . . perhaps marital problems. We as Christians can usually best reach people who have suffered less than, or the same as, we, not those who have suffered more. God has placed each of us exactly where He pleases on the scale of suffering. But remember, He reserves the right to move us up or down that scale any time He chooses in order to open up to us new avenues of ministry.

Two years ago I was sharing my testimony at a country church in southern Pennsylvania. After the service as I sat chatting with several members of the congregation, I kept noticing a tall and rather handsome man standing in the background with his family. Eventually he eased up to my chair. "Joni, excuse me, my name is Doug Sorzano. I just wanted to tell you that I wish I could understand and appreciate what you're going through. You see, I've never known what it means to be paralyzed or face a really traumatic accident. I have a lovely wife and beautiful kids—in fact, they're right here. Let me introduce you."

Between introductions he managed to tell me how deeply impressed and excited he felt over all that had been said and done that evening. But he was honest in that he did not pretend to know and fully grasp all I had experienced. He was one who could not say, "I know exactly how you feel."

Riding home later in our van, my traveling companions and I prayed that God might use what I had said to help some people.

Weeks passed in which I busied myself with drawing, reading, and an occasional speaking engagement.

One afternoon, perhaps a month later, I received a phone call from a neighbor of the Sorzano family who had been in church that evening in Pennsylvania. She had called to let me know about "something awful that had happened."

"It was just last Saturday, Joni. Doug has always been a motorcycle buff and spent lots of his free time riding trails. And, I'll tell you, he's good. But this time he and his buddies decided to tackle a new area of the woods."

"Go on," I added hesitantly.

"Well, from what we can gather there was a quick turn in the path. Anyway, apparently Doug came up suddenly on a hidden log. The front wheel of his bike hit it, and he was thrown some distance. . . ."

I was listening intently, but my imagination ran ahead of what my ears were hearing. Scared to ask, but wanting to know, I interrupted her with a question.

"Is he . . . uh . . . that is, has he—"

Reading my thoughts, she answered me in midsentence.

"His neck's broken."

There was an awkward silence.

The shock stunned me and made my ears ring. I was glad she couldn't see my eyes fill with tears and my face becoming flushed and heated. Getting hold of myself, I tried to speak, but didn't know exactly what to say. All I could do finally was assure her I would call or write this family very soon and let them know I would be praying for them in this time of real struggle.

After we hung up, my memory desperately tried to scramble back and recall my brief conversation with Doug. "I've never faced a really traumatic accident, Joni . . . have a lovely wife and beautiful kids . . . I wish I could understand what you're going through. . . ."

I later learned that this man was paralyzed from the shoulder level down, confused, and frustrated.

My sister, Jay, grabbed a pen and some stationery and came into the room to help me write a letter to Doug and his family. But what do you say to a guy who has just broken his neck? Give advice? No, not just yet. Share some Scriptures? Okay, but it sure would be good to say something more personal. What does a person really want when he's hurting? I guess he wants love . . . and to be understood. *That's it. He wants someone to know just what it is that he's going through. And I can do that.*

I am so glad that as I wrote that letter I was able to comfort Doug with real empathy. My own paralysis enabled me to walk in his shoes and see things from his point of view. It allowed me to honestly say, "I know exactly how you feel."

There is a healing balm in those words, but only if they are made believable by our own experience of suffering. People know whether or not we really understand them. They can look into our lives and see whether or not we have experienced deep anguish. If we say "I know how you feel" glibly, our words are empty, hollow statements. But if we can say it in sincerity, it can be such a comfort.

Jesus Himself came to earth partially to answer the charges that heaven's "ivory palaces" kept Him from knowing the pains of mankind. "Because He Himself suffered when He was tested, He can help others when they're tested . . . We have a High Priest who can sympathize with our weaknesses" (Heb. 2:18, 4:15 Beck Translation). If He endured hardship in order to relate to those who suffer, we can expect to do no less. Therefore, I have learned to view the breaking of my neck as a special act of God that helps me relate to and comfort people in similar conditions.*

* * * *

So far I have been speaking about relating to people who must cope with difficulties that are higher on the scale of suffering than ours. These are people who face death, paralysis, and bankruptcy, to name just a few. But this is not the whole story.

Some months after my accident, I started to notice that the small, everyday difficulties my friends and relatives experienced—broken fingernails, dental bills, hay fever, and dented car fenders—were every bit as real to them as my immobility was to me. It began to strike me that there is something universal about suffering. In the first place, everyone experiences it; no one is exempt. But in the second place, no matter how much or how little one must endure,

---

*At this time of publication, Doug Sorzano has adjusted marvelously to his paralysis. In speaking with him over the phone, I learned that he is presently sharing his faith with others who are in his condition. The Sorzanos live in Kennett Square, Pennsylvania, and attend church at Willowdale Chapel.

everyone finds suffering unpleasant. An irksome housefly can momentarily rob a person of joy every bit as much as a broken leg in a cast.

And so, because everyone knows something about problems and pain, we can be certain the Bible is speaking to *all* of us when it speaks about suffering, no matter how much or how little we have had to endure. God's grace is just as sufficient for a paralytic as it is for a boy who doesn't make the baseball team. And the same godly response is as necessary to the happiness of a housewife whose cake has flopped as it is to a patient dying of leukemia.

All this tells us something important about being a help to others who suffer. Although having the same problem as someone else helps us to feel with them, we can still be of immense encouragement to those who suffer more than we do. That's because we need the same kind of grace to handle our little problems as they do to handle the big ones. Let me give you an example of this.

I live on a beautiful farm in central Maryland where we are surrounded by rolling green hills and pastures. The countryside is dotted with time-honored barns, sheds, and spring-houses built decades ago.

On our farm there was such a building, a beautiful old barn erected long ago by Pennsylvania Dutch builders who obviously knew their craft. It had weathered countless storms and had seen generations come and go. My father loved the old barn, and there he made a workshop where he fashioned many original creations out of wood, leather, and metal.

But about five years ago on a summer Friday night something happened to change all of that. My sister Kathy, her husband Butch, and I were settled down in our dining room just talking and killing time, long after dinner. While Butch lazily picked his guitar, occasionally one of us would glance up at the stars through the open picture window. Outside, the chirping of crickets and other country sounds gave no sign of any disturbance. Even the distant screeching of tires along the narrow road that winds in front of our house barely captured our attention; young people do occasionally race their cars there.

But on this night, instead of passing the house and fading in the distance, the screeching stopped at the paddock of our barn. The abrupt silence brought an inquisitive look to Butch's face, our eyes met briefly, and the guitar became quiet. Kathy walked over to the window, unsuccessfully straining to see through the darkness. The only movement came from a moth flickering around the lamp.

In a moment, the car sped off.

It wasn't long before Kathy thought she could see a flicker of light . . . then another.

"Joni! Butch!" she screamed suddenly. "The barn's on fire!"

Butch raced for the phone and fumbled through the directory trying to find the number for the fire department. I, of course, couldn't help but watched as Kathy dashed out the door, then down the pasture toward the barn. Butch quickly followed.

By this time the roaring blaze illuminated the whole area. Up through the old roof curled pillars of black smoke. By the time the fire department was able to get there, it was too late. Within an hour the barn was reduced to smoking ruins.

It was so sad to see my dad, a little, seventy-two-year-old arthritic man, shuffling through the smoldering ash and rubble the next day. Overturning charred objects with slight kicks of his toe, he searched for anything he might be able to salvage from the antiques and tools he had saved over the years. His only compensation was the old stone foundation. It, at least, had withstood the fiery test.

But dad didn't complain or get depressed because his beautiful barn had burnt to the ground. Instead, he jumped right in and got to work. No pouting, no second-guessing about God's purposes. Within two months dad had erected a new barn, a real testimony to his uncomplaining spirit and persevering faith.

Unbelievable as it may seem, two years later our family was forced to relive the same ordeal. Another summer night; another fire! The cause of the flame this time was unknown, but the results were the same. Again there were the sirens and flashing lights from the fire trucks. Again neighbors had to hold the horses back from running through the fences in fear. Once more the intense heat kept the surrounding crowd at a distance and singed the leaves of nearby trees. And once more dad picked up the pieces and started over again, trusting that God knew what He was doing.

My sisters and I were simply amazed at our father's faith in God's sovereignty. I, in particular, benefited from observing his strength of character.

That my dad could encourage me at that point should teach us something. The financial and sentimental loss he suffered in those fires was very real. But it was less than what I suffered when I broke my neck. (If any of you doubt that, ask yourself, "Would I rather lose some material object of great financial and sentimental value or break my neck and be paralyzed for life?") Dad has never been paralyzed and, therefore, cannot say to me, "I know what you're going through." His trials measured lower on the scale of suffering than mine. But the way he handled them taught me a lot. His uncomplaining attitude and refusal to be angry at God convinced me that *a Christian does not always have to suffer in the same manner, or to the same degree, as his fellow-Christians to be a real help to them.*

Sitting at a distance watching my dad again pick through the rubble and again rebuild his barn reminded me once more that all of us fit onto a scale of suffering, some higher and some lower. God does give some of us especially difficult burdens to carry so that we can honestly say to others in the same boat, "I know how you feel." But it's also true that by being faithful to God in our lesser frustrations, we can comfort and reach even people who suffer far more than we do.

I think the apostle Paul had this in mind when he said it all so concisely long ago:

> Praise be to the God and Father of our Lord Jesus Christ, the Father of compassion and the God of all comfort, who comforts us in all our troubles, so that we can comfort those in any trouble with the comfort we ourselves have received from God. (2 Cor. 1:3-4).

2 Body Building

Have you ever noticed how the things in life that have the greatest potential for good also have an unusual potential for bad? Take fire, for instance, one of man's greatest discoveries. The same flame that cooks a steak can also ruin acres of precious forest within a matter of minutes—or burn down a barn. And what about sex? It, too, can be very good and very bad. Although God meant it to bind husbands and wives together, give them pleasure, and bring them children, its misuse brings guilt, heartache, and tears.

So it is with suffering. While it is God's choicest tool to mold our character, it also has the tendency to breed selfcenteredness. I've wasted hours pitying myself and getting all wrapped up in imagining that my broken neck was God's way of getting even with me for my sins, when in reality He was far from being "out to get me." In fact, though at the time it did not occur to me, the whole ordeal of my paralysis was inspired by His love. And not only love for me, but love for those around me, for one of God's goals in our trials is to help us not only feel with one another, but actually build each other up.

This particular lesson was made very real to me during the winter of 1975. The pastor of a large Baptist church in Wichita, Kansas, had asked me to come and speak during his church's annual missionary conference. I accepted eagerly. For one thing, I was just beginning to travel and so the idea of getting on a plane to go anywhere to talk to anybody was really exciting. But also, it was the first missions conference I had ever attended, let alone participated in. I didn't know a great deal about missions, nor had I sat and talked at length with any missionaries. For all I knew they spent most of their time trekking through the jungles, fighting off snakes with their machetes. My traveling companions on that trip, Sherry and Julie, didn't know any more than I did. So as the three of us sat on the back row of that large and crowded church, we eagerly soaked in all we could from the missionary speakers on the program. Who knew? They might even tell some cannibal stories!

But do you know what we learned? They were people just like us! Listening to them tell of their daily struggles and victories in such far-off places as Brazil, Japan, and the Philippines made us aware of our responsibility to them. After all, though we lived thousands of miles apart, we were one with them in what the Bible calls the "body of Christ." This really hit home as Christians who had escaped from Communist Rumania told the conference just how heavily believers behind the Iron Curtain count on our prayers. I so appreciated these missionaries sharing with us that I looked forward to the closing service on Sunday evening when I would have the chance to share with them in turn.

But missionaries weren't the only ones we met that week. We had sat with a number of the church's young people each night and had become close friends. So when none of us wanted to part company after the Saturday night meeting, we decided to go to an ice cream parlor together. What fun being with that group at 11:00 P.M., joking and kidding with one another!

After finishing our milkshakes and paying the bill, Sherry helped put me in my coat, and we all stepped out into the January night air. Ever since my diving accident, my body's "thermostat" hasn't worked very well, so I'm not able to adjust easily to extremes in temperature. Since the parking lot was deserted by this time, I asked Sherry to tilt the chair back and run us across to the car in order to escape the cold.

Two shadowy figures glided in the darkness across the smooth asphalt sea, whooping and laughing, navigating a course toward the distant lighthouse that was a streetlight. The dark seemed innocent enough, without hint of anything sinister. With friendly images of laughter and ice cream still dancing in our minds, what reason had we to suppose that anything but safety lay between us and the car? Who would have guessed the blackness of the night concealed a patch of ice on the pavement just feet in front of us?

A gasp escaped from Sherry as her heel slipped beneath her, causing the chair to swerve and careen up on one wheel. Face forward, I went flying into the air. Being paralyzed, I could not even use my hands to cushion the fall. Seeing the pavement rushing toward my face gave me only a split second to grimace and tightly shut my eyes.

I felt my face strike the asphalt and discovered that getting hit solidly like that can literally cause one to see stars. My body seemed to bounce on the surface and rolled near the front of our Ford wagon.

"Oh, no!" I heard Sherry exclaim.

It's strange, but when something like this happens, everything seems to go into slow motion. You

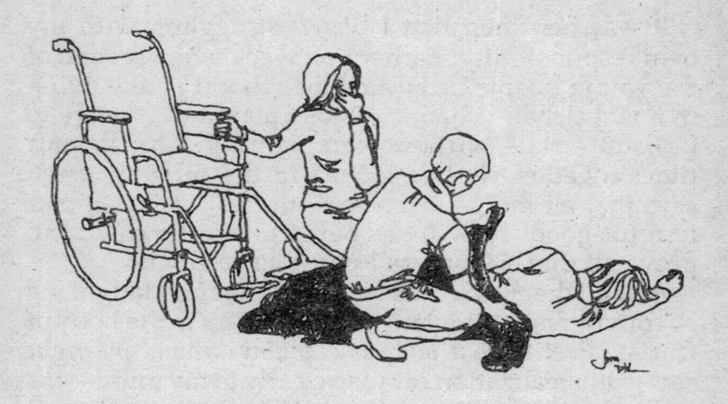

hear every sound very clearly. Everything presses indelibly on your mind.

There was muffled talking. "Come on over here, Sherry." Shoes sounded on the pavement as someone led her away. A cash box clattered . . . coins rolling . . . money from my cards and drawings we had sold that night. "Ooh, she's got blood all over her face!" screamed one girl.

The young people began to crowd around now, but I had to tightly shut my eyes to keep out the blood. I remember moving my neck slightly to make sure it hadn't been broken, running my tongue over my teeth to check if any had been knocked out, moving my jaw to confirm that it wasn't fractured.

Immediately someone knelt near me and cradled my head in her hands on her lap. It was Julie. "Are you okay?" she managed. I opened my eyes just long enough to see her brush the hair out of my face; her hands were wet with blood. She kept asking me if I was okay, and I just nodded. Stifled sobs made me aware that she was trying to hide her crying from me. In spite of her tears, she felt it her responsibility to keep calm and stable.

It was just then that I began struggling with my own responsibility. Earlier that week when several of the young people had asked me what it is like living in a wheelchair, I had tried to explain how we are to face our trials without complaining. During our times together we had looked in the Bible where it says that all things, even hard things, fit into a pattern for good. Now I was being given the chance to prove all that. How was I going to respond?

And all that week those missionaries had taught me so convincingly about my duty to others in the body of Christ. *Part of that body is standing around me right now*—the realization came so clearly to my mind—*the youth group and all the others. What about them?*

But my selfish nature didn't want to be bothered with "them." It only cared about itself, old number one. And right now, old number one was freezing cold and hurting badly.

How come it's me that has to go through this? Haven't I already suffered more than most of these people standing around? Why can't God use somebody else to be the visual aid for His object lesson?

I knew such thinking wasn't right. But it's hard to put God and others above one's self, especially when you're in pain.

Who cares what everyone thinks about how I handle this situation? It's MY face that's all banged up. And why'd I have to get hurt above my neck–the only place on my whole body I can feel?!

Almost at once the Holy Spirit began taking up the challenge in answer to my questions. I was reminded of God's Word: "Do you not know that your body is a temple of the Holy Spirit. . . ? You are not your own; you were bought at a price. Therefore, honor God with your body" (1 Cor. 6:19-20).

Who cared how I responded? *God* cared. Did I really have the right to complain about my injured face? No. My body was not my own; it was God's to do with as He pleased. He bought it with His own Son's blood.

My first responsibility was to honor God by showing these onlooking friends in practice what I had shared with them in theory—that there are no accidents in a Christian's life. If God has sent something, it must be for our ultimate good.

Or the good of those around us, I reasoned. *Wow! Sometimes as Christians we're just not given any choice in the matter. If we care at all, we have to handle things God's way.*

Lying there, I knew what I needed to do. So for what seemed to be the ten-thousandth time in my life, as an act of my will, I grimaced and then quietly thanked God for what was happening. *Dear God, thanks for what's going on right now. . . . Don't let me get angry. These kids are watching. . . . Let them learn how to handle their tough times by seeing how I handle this. And please . . . You get the glory.*

Eventually, I knew, God would get glory in some way from this incident. But I hadn't realized He would begin doing it immediately. God was evident in the love and concern each person there showed for me. Everyone selflessly piled their coats on me for protection from the cold. Realizing I was still uncomfortable, one man knelt and held me close to him for warmth, whispering, "Everything's going to be all right." Others piled into the car to pray. One called for an ambulance and another notified the pastor of the church we were visiting.

The rest of that eventful night was spent getting X-rays, having my forehead stitched, and lying awake from the pain of a concussion and a broken nose. During those painful, sleepless hours I had plenty of time to think. *Thanks for not letting me fall apart, God.*

Eventually I was released and driven back to our hotel room. In the wee hours of the morning I finally dozed off to sleep with difficulty, needing to be wakened every two hours to check on my concussion.

The next morning a bit before 11:00 I was awakened by the sound of the hair dryer in the bathroom. Peeking her head around the door, Sherry asked with a hesitant smile, "How ya doin'?"

"Well, I . . . ooh. . . ." I began to answer, but the pain immediately reminded me of the spill I had taken the night before. Physically, I wasn't doing all that great. The stitches hurt, the headache throbbed, I hadn't gotten much sleep, and my face was bruised and swollen. But internally I was in an okay frame of mind. "I'm doing pretty good I guess. What's up?"

"We thought we'd wake you up in time for a little late morning TV," Julie piped in, adjusting the antenna. "The pastor told us we could catch the church service right here since it's televised every week."

So they propped me up with pillows, and we watched eagerly. After the choir anthem, the pastor made a special announcement. "We're sorry to announce that Miss Joni Eareckson had a spill last night resulting in a broken nose and a number of stitches. Last night as we talked in the emergency room I suggested she cancel her engagement with us this evening, but she insists she'll feel up to it. We're asking all of you to join us in prayer for her."

I was glad someone was praying for me. But as I leaned back on the pillows, I couldn't help but smile. After all, the *real* crisis was over—the one inside me.

Wheeling into the packed-out assembly that evening momentarily took my breath away. Chairs filled the aisles, and people were standing up in the back and scrunched in the choir loft. I decided not to use the carefully prepared notes and illustrations I had gotten together weeks ago. Instead, I shared some Scriptures that had to do with what happened the night before.

"One of the best things we can do for our brothers and sisters in Christ is to gain victory in our own trials." The small lapel mike picked up my words and projected them to the audience.

"The Book of Ephesians makes it clear that we are to care for other Christians *because* we are one with them. Believers are never told to *become* one; we *already are* one and are expected to act like it.

"You know, First Corinthians 12 says that together we Christians are like a human body, with Christ as the head. The human body is perhaps the most amazing example of teamwork anywhere in the world. Every part needs the other. When the stomach is hungry, the eyes spot the hamburger, the feet run to the snack stand, and the hands douse it with mustard and shove it into the mouth where it goes back down to the stomach. Now that's cooperation!"

Chuckles rose from the audience.

"So we can see why passages like Ephesians 4:16 tell us that we Christians affect one another spiritually by what we are and do individually. No organ in a body can act without affecting all the rest. A sprained ankle immobilizes the entire person; and the hands that catch a winning touchdown pass bring honor to the whole body. There is something almost mystical about the intricate link between us as believers. Your failures, are my failures, and your victories, mine."

No one was moving. Everyone listened intently. It was obvious that people were getting the message.

I continued, "Therefore, if we care anything about Christ—the head of the body—and other Christians—the rest of the body—we must face our problems with them in mind. God helped Julie and me do just that last night. She was an example to me. I was an example to others. God wants to do the same thing through you."

And so the Lord used my injuries from the previous night as a grand platform from which to share His all-wise plan in allowing His children to endure pain for their good and His glory.

* * * *

About a year later I received a letter from Steve, written during a time when I was traveling a lot and was a little homesick. His encouraging words were an excellent summary of what I learned the night I broke my nose in the parking lot. I was reminded again that our sufferings, far from giving us a license for self-pity, give us an excellent opportunity to teach and build up others. Here is a portion of that letter:

> So, Joni, when you've got to speak ten times in one week, when your jaw gets a little tired from smiling at well-wishers, when your back aches, when you've got a secret inner urge sometime to be on your feet but feel you can't express it 'cause the folks around you would take it wrong, when you miss your friends, when the Bible seems boring, when you feel insecure, when you find sinful thoughts and attitudes creeping into your head, when you're tempted to run mental movies of your success and glory in yourself—in short . . . when you feel like carrying a smooth cross and slipping a bit, even "just for today" . . . don't. Don't be discouraged, and don't sin. And don't feel the hassle is in vain, because you honestly have got to be one of the mainstays in my life when it comes to setting an example when I feel like quitting.

We are onstage. Others are watching. We can do our part well, building up the entire audience. Or we can ad-lib by acting out our own bitter feelings and bring dishonor to the Playwright. The choice is ours.

3 I Wouldn't Do This For Just Anybody!

We people sometimes like to brag about how great and wonderful we are, but when we're unexpectedly given the chance to prove it, we often have trouble making good our words. A recent cartoon illustrated this in a clever way. During a college football game a middle-aged fan seated on the front bleacher kept hurling snide remarks at the coach and players on the losing team. His wisecracks were obviously intended to impress those seated around him with his prowess and knowledge of the game. When the frustrated coach finally had his fill of abuse, he turned to the stands, pointed a finger, and barked, "You with all the advice, go in for Oblonsky!" Gulp! He sure popped that fan's balloon.

Men often have to back down when challenged to support their boastful words with actions. But God, unlike our friend in the bleachers, never has to back down. In fact, because He really *is* great and wonderful, He's always looking for an opportunity to demonstrate that greatness to mankind. Human suffering provides one of the best platforms from which to do this.

Of course, the most obvious way God uses suffering to glorify Himself is to miraculously remove that suffering. Jesus went about restoring sight to the blind, healing the lepers, raising the dead, and doing all sorts of awesome things to ease human misery. Sure enough, as a result, "When the multitudes saw it, they marvelled, and glorified God" (Matt. 9:8 KJV).

But what about today? Jesus is no longer with us in bodily form, walking the hills of Judea, doing the things He once did. Though God still can, and sometimes does, step in to do things in a miraculous way, that is no longer His usual method. Today God has a second, less obvious but not less powerful, way of using suffering to glorify Himself.

Strange as it may seem, it appears God often not only allows, but actually insures that His children undergo and endure long periods of real difficulty.[1] Not only that, but He seems to be hurting His own cause by letting this take place within plain view of unbelievers who scoff at Christianity. Not one embarrassing detail escapes the eyes of these scorners as they jeer, "Look at how this so-called loving God treats His devoted followers!"

But wait. As we continue observing, we notice something unusual. These Christians, on whom God has sent trial after trial, refuse to complain. Rather than shake rebellious fists at heaven, and rather than curse the One who allows them such misery, they respond with praise to their Creator.

At first the world mocks. "It's only a phase," they assure themselves. "Just wait." But as the trials continue and the Christians refuse to "curse God and die," the watching world is forced to swallow its own words and eventually drop its jaw in amazed disbelief.

Thus, *God has shown one of the most effective ways in which suffering can bring glory to Himself—it demonstrates His ability to maintain the loyalty of His people even when they face difficult trials.* If being a Christian brought us nothing but ease and comfort, the world wouldn't learn anything very impressive about our God. "Big deal," men would say. "Anybody can get a following by waiting on people hand and foot." But when a Christian shows faith and love for his Maker in spite of the fact that, on the surface, it looks as if he's been forgotten, it does say something impressive. It shows the scoffers that our God is worth serving even when the going gets tough. It lets a skeptical world know that what the Christian has is real.

I can recall meeting a girl some time ago at a bookstore in California who is a perfect example of what I mean. The store was situated in an affluent neighborhood, filled that day with homemakers and nicely dressed children with polished faces—a pleasant place to be. A line had formed as people waited to meet me or have their books and prints autographed.

As I took a pen in my mouth to sign someone's book, my ears caught a sound that seemed out of place in the general chattering and bustling going on around the room. Sneaking a glance over the top of the book which was being held before me, I discovered the source.

There, in a wheelchair at the back of the line, sat a seriously deformed young woman whose inability to mouth words resulted in rather loud, distorted grunting and groaning sounds. In the various hospitals where I'd stayed I had met many people whose speech was similarly affected by disease. I guessed that she was the victim of that horrible crippler known as cerebral palsy and found out later this was the case.

As she approached, I couldn't help noticing that her hands were shaking, her feet were twisted and gnarled, and she was drooling from lack of control over her mouth. Matted hair crowned her head, and an unevenly buttoned blouse suggested she was hard to dress. Her handicap had made her unpleasant to look at, to say the least.

I recalled the time when being around such a person would have made me uncomfortable. I used to want nothing to do with anyone whose handicap seemed only to underscore and remind me of my condition. But God had long ago helped me overcome feelings like that, and I was anxious to meet her.

"Joni, I'd like you to meet Nadine," her nurse introduced us as she wheeled the young woman's chair next to mine. In the conversation that followed, during which the nurse interpreted as best she could, I learned Nadine was a Christian and the same age as I. Though her physical appearance might have given the distinct impression that Nadine was retarded, she actually was an intelligent, well-read person who enjoyed composing poetry as a hobby.

That afternoon Nadine presented me with a letter expressing appreciation for some thoughts I had shared in my book. But then she gave me a real treasure—a small plaque consisting of a poem and some angels clipped from the front of Christmas cards. Nadine had cut out the angels using the toes of her "good" foot to operate a pair of scissors. That was several years ago, and I still have it hanging in my home.

As Nadine was talking, my mind flipped back through the pages of philosophy and other books I had read during my days of searching and skepticism in the hospital. "Either God has the love to remove human misery but doesn't have the power," they argued, "or He has the power but not the love. Or perhaps He has neither. But He certainly doesn't have both."

You would think an argument like that would hit right to the heart of a thinking person such as Nadine. She is institutionalized in a nursing home and will probably never enjoy the comforts of living with close friends or family who care. She will probably never marry or experience any number of things the world considers essential for happiness. Why doesn't she curse her all-powerful, all-loving God for treating her so? She should be one of the most depressed persons on earth, full of despair and purposelessness. No one would blame her. At best she should be a resigned stoic, determined to bravely bear her lot in life and to stifle all emotions.

But conversing with Nadine for almost an hour convinced me that she hasn't gotten that message! Nadine knows what it means to experience the joy of the Lord, the "peace that passes all understanding." She can identify with Paul when he says, "Though outwardly we are wasting away, yet inwardly we are being renewed day by day" (2 Cor. 4:16).

And what is most interesting, she not only tolerates God—she *loves* Him. The God she has come to know is so worth knowing, so real, that she gladly and willingly endures her condition if that's what pleases Him.

Does Nadine's suffering glorify God? It sure does. Why? Because God miraculously removes it? No, her suffering glorifies God because the people who see and know her are forced to at least consider the fact that Nadine's Lord must be somebody special to inspire such loyalty. I thought to myself, *If anybody ever wants some evidence of what God's grace and power can do in a life, then they should see this woman.*

Sometimes skeptics will look at people like Nadine and try to deny that God is the real source of that Christian's inner peace. To them, all of this talk about heaven, God, and the joy of the Lord is mere escapism, a mental cop-out, a refusal to face reality. From time to time I myself have been accused of using faith in God as a psychological crutch.

When this happens, I merely point to the facts: It's hard enough for someone who's always been an indoor bookworm sort of person to adjust to a wheelchair life style. But most people agree that it's even harder for someone, such as myself, who's been very active. As a high school student I was always on the go—riding horses, playing field hockey, driving around in my sports car, doing crazy stunts. "When I was on my feet, I couldn't sit still for a minute," I often tell people. "Now I have to sit still for the rest of my life."

No mere set of dos and don'ts, no speculative religious philosophy dreamed up in my head, no belief in a vague and all-supreme First Cause, no creed about God could sustain and give me peace in this chair. And certainly such things could not make me actually rejoice in my condition. Either I must be mad, or there is a living God behind all of this who is more than just a theological axiom. He is personal, and He works and proves Himself in my life. And this has made many people think twice about Him.

I think I know what some of you who are Christians are wondering at this point: "My, it's exciting how God is using people like Joni and Nadine to glorify Himself. But I don't have any serious handicaps. My life is pretty normal. What about me?" If that's your thinking, please don't imagine that your trials need to be as traumatic as Nadine's or mine to be of real value to God. Accepting the everyday strains of life with a joyful heart can have the same effect on a smaller scale.

I think of my sister, Jay, and my friends, Betsy and Sheryl, who often travel with me. Let me tell you, these women know something about the everyday strains of life! In the first place, they care for all my physical needs, and if you've never cared for a paralytic while traveling, you don't know how much work it can be. Many mornings, in order to have me ready for an early meeting, they need to be up out of their hotel beds at 5:00 A.M. After getting themselves ready comes the hour-and-a-half-long process of getting me up, exercising me, bathing and dressing me, brushing my teeth, washing my hair, and so on.

But that's not all. Whenever we drive, I also need to be lifted out of my chair and into the car. This involves one of the girls leaning over my back and lifting my body from the waist up while another carries me by the legs. After being squeezed into the seat I need to be readjusted, positioned, and strapped in while someone folds down my collapsible chair and fits it into the trunk of the car. I'm not about to tell you exactly how much I weigh, but since I can't move myself, I can be pretty heavy dead weight! When we arrive, the process has to be reversed as I'm taken out of the car and placed back in my chair. On a recent trip to Minneapolis, Betsy, Sheryl, and Jay had to place me in and out of the car fifteen times in one day!

And there's an emotional strain they often have to put up with when we travel together. I'm talking about the insensitivity that a few people sometimes show by treating me like a queen and almost totally ignoring my sister and friends.

Arising early to get me ready, lifting me in and out of the car, being ignored by others—perhaps you wouldn't even call these things actual "trials" like Nadine's and my handicap. But when people see the way these women endure their small but real frustrations with an uncomplaining heart of love, it points their attention to God, and He is glorified.

In a sense, people like Nadine and my sister and friends are modern-day Jobs. You remember how Job was a righteous man, blessed by God with all sorts of material comforts. The praise he gave the Lord in return disgusted Satan. "He just serves You because You bless him," Satan jeered at God. "If You'd take away his family and possessions, he'd curse You to Your face." The implication was, "It's Your blessings he loves, not You, God. You're not great enough to get someone to follow You on Your own merits."

And so God allowed Satan to test Job. Job lost his money, his health, and most of his family. "Curse God and die," his wife urged him. But he refused. With unbelievable loyalty he cried, "Though he slay me, yet will I hope in him" (Job 13:15 NIV).

What a testimony! The statement speaks highly of Job, but even more highly of God who is able to inspire His servants' loyalty despite their toughest trials. It is the Old Testament equivalent of Paul's statement in Philippians: "What is more, I consider everything a loss compared to the surpassing greatness of knowing Christ Jesus my Lord, for whose sake I have lost all things. I consider them rubbish, that I may gain Christ." (Phil. 3:8).

I really don't mind the inconvenience of being paralyzed if my faithfulness to God while in this wheelchair will bring glory to Him. Have you considered the potential glory your life can give to God if, in *your* "wheelchair," you remain faithful?

4 Unlikely Saints!

A dreadful silence momentarily seized the great banquet hall of the renowned Fairbairn Castle. Not the slightest puff of wind rippled the colorful banners along the massive, grey stone walls. Over the huge medieval fireplace hung the royal family's coat of arms; and, as if in symbolic defiance, on the opposite wall was mounted the standard of the neighboring Duke Einar. Tension had been building for months between these two powers, and the duke's evil intention to overthrow the prince had been verbally challenged during this annual feast held for the lords and ladies of the entire kingdom.

Poised in crouched readiness on the wooden banquet table was the strong figure of Prince Eric. In his fist was clutched the pearl-inlaid handle of his sword, the weapon his father, the king, had passed on to him during these final days of the king's life. The sleek blade reflected a ray of sunlight stretching through the window in the thick castle wall. It was the finest sword in the land.

On the floor, surrounding the prince like sharks around their prey, paced three of the duke's henchmen, swords drawn, awaiting a split second to catch

Eric off his guard. The prince's eyes flashed from one to the other, watching to see who would strike first.

Suddenly, the sound of steel meeting steel! Two of the soldiers rushed the prince, but he parried their blows with his sword, deftly avoiding each stab and thrusting with plunges of his own.

A stab . . . a wound . . . blood. One of the duke's soldiers fell to the floor, his sword dropping from his hand. But the prince could not take a second to glory in this partial victory; he swerved to continue meeting the other two.

Now a man was on each side of him. As he dealt with the blows from the enemy to his right, he stole a glance over his left shoulder, checking his position. But in doing so, his grip on his sword loosened slightly and the magnificent weapon was knocked from his hand.

A gasp escaped from the crowd. Ladies lining the outer wall drew their handkerchiefs to their open mouths, and each observer lost his breath in horror.

But wait! With deer-like speed the prince leaped beyond the range of their blades, pulled his dagger out of his belt, and grabbed the brass candlestick holder that decorated the table.

With two to one odds and armed with frightfully inferior weapons, he again sprang into the battle, diverting blows with the lamp and dealing them with his dagger. Ducking as a side thrust barely missed his head, he came back up, dodging the swing of his opponent, and delivered a deathblow to the heart of the second soldier.

The stunned survivor of the duke's force looked on in wide-eyed fear. He and Eric circled one another in silence. At the peak of tension, the soldier struck.

A hair-thin line streaked Eric's sleeve and turned crimson as blood seeped from the wound. The prince retreated, step after step, until he was finally pinned

against the wall. His puny tools were no match for the sophisticated sword of his opponent. The blows came quicker. Soon he must fall.

Suddenly his opponent made his thrust. Eric jumped to the left, and the lunge aimed at his heart merely grazed his side and struck the wall. But before the duke's soldier could pull in his sword and resume his stance, Eric slapped the blade downward with his lamp and sent his dagger flying forward.

The soldier gripped the knife which lay buried in the flesh of his shoulder, put up his other hand as if to say, "No more," and conceded the victory to Eric. The joyful crowd swarmed around the prince and offered loud and hearty congratulations. They began to chant a song which became a classic for generations—

"With the sword of the king, Prince Eric is strong,

But the knife and the lamp prove him mightier still!"

* * * *

I love to read adventure stories like this one about adventure story? It is the fascinating account of how the evil villain, Satan, enslaved the citizens of the
the evil villain, Satan, enslaved the citizens of the
Kingdom of Earth through treachery and deceit—how he usurped the authority of the rightful Ruler (who is good and just) and set up his own rival government. Furthermore, it is the story of how the good Ruler sent His only Son to invade Satan's territory, free the captive subjects, and retake the kingdom under the family banner.

If I were God, how would I have gotten the job done? Well, first I would probably pick the smartest men and women possible to be on my strategy team—the Ph.D.'s, the college professors. Then I would draft the world's sharpest businessmen and millionaires to finance the operation. My public relations people would be the most effective communicators to be found anywhere, tops in their field. To qualify even as a mere rank-and-file member of my organization, a person would have to be young, athletic, and unusually attractive.

Weak people need not apply. Those with physical defects? Forget it. People who might slow down my progress? Never. Those to whom the world is not naturally attracted? Someone who might jeopardize my reputation? No way. A man or woman whose life is filled with problems? Not on your life. I would accept only the cream of the crop.

But thank God I'm not running the world—He is! And He opens His arms wide to the poor, the sick, the ugly, the lonely, the weak, the ungifted, the unlovely, the unlikely. That's because of His great love. It's also because what's in a person's heart matters more to Him than what's on the outside.

But there's still another reason, a very special one, why God accepts and uses those He does. And the key can be found in the story of Prince Eric. Do you remember the words the people sang about him?

"With the sword of the king, Prince Eric is strong,

But the knife and the lamp prove him mightier still!"

Any struggle between a hero and "the bad guys" is interesting enough in itself. But when the hero is suddenly disadvantaged, as when Eric lost his sword, a new element is introduced. Now the hero is in far more danger than before. He has less chance of winning. But if by sheer ability he overcomes in spite of the odds, he ends up twice as much of a hero because he won using weak and inferior weapons.

All through the Bible God shows us that this is exactly the way He does things to bring maximum glory to Himself. The apostle Paul told the Corinthian Christians to look around at themselves and realize that, on the whole, God called people into their fellowship who by human standards were neither wise, nor influential, nor of noble birth. He's saying that God deliberately chooses weak, suffering, and unlikely candidates to get His work done so that when the job is accomplished, the glory goes to Him and not to us. Think of it! The very weakness and problems we find so painful are just what He uses to honor Himself. We are not a pearl-inlaid sword in His hand. We are a dagger and a candlestick holder doing a sword's job!

When I first got out of the hospital in 1969, two years after I broke my neck, I was in a state of deep depression. There I was, only nineteen years old and with nothing to look forward to but a lifetime of sitting in a wheelchair. I knew in a vague sort of way that the Bible probably contained the answers for my situation somewhere between its covers, but I desperately needed someone to show me exactly where and what some of those answers were.

Even so, not just anybody could have approached me with religious advice and expected to win my interest and respect. You understand. I had been into the high school scene—played on Woodlawn's field hockey team, was a member of the National Honor Society, dated the captain of the football team from a neighboring high school. For someone to get my attention back then, they usually had to be sort of intellectual, athletic, or popular.

Now you'd think God would have packaged His answers for me in some tall, tanned youth director who ran a "surfboard ministry" down at Ocean City. *He* would have caught my attention. Or maybe I would have been impressed by some brainy seminary student in an Ivy League suit. Perhaps if Billy Graham had held a "Greater Woodlawn Crusade" —maybe that would have inspired me.

But, no. Do you know who God sent? A tall, lanky, sixteen-year-old boy with a paper route. An unlikely candidate, wouldn't you say? By my standards, this guy really missed the mark. I mean, here was no super youth director or intellectual seminary student. He was just a teen-ager—only with a big, black Bible. But I was listening! And God used the long hours I spent with Steve Estes, a high school junior, to lift my spirits and help me understand God's Word. It was almost as though God delighted in displaying His power through another kid rather than sending some Bible scholar trained in counseling handicapped people.

Today as Steve and I think back to those early days of our friendship, we laugh and wonder at how God used such an unlikely relationship to begin turning my life around. But when you think about it, that shouldn't surprise us. He whittled Gideon's 32,000-man army down to 300 before sending them out to fight hordes of Midianites. He sent a teen-age shepherd boy, David, to do battle with Goliath, the seasoned warrior-giant of the Philistines. He gave Abraham a barren wife, Sarah, after promising him a nation of descendants as numerous as the stars of heaven. Why? So that when the Midianites were routed, Goliath had fallen, and Sarah had given birth to a son, the world would know that God, not man, had done it.

And that's where suffering comes in. It drives us to our knees in weakness and frailty. And don't we see that that's just where God wants us? For then His strength is most obvious.

If ever there was anyone who knew the value of being weak, it was the apostle Paul. In fact, he took up most of his second letter to the Corinthians to argue the fact that *God uses weak people*.

It seems there were all kinds of phony apostles running around trying to shoot down Paul's ministry and build up their own. They droned on and on, bragging about their fantastic accomplishments, glorious visions, and successful ministries.

"What about you, Paul?" they jeered. "Can you top what we've done?"[2]

So Paul answered them. "You want me to boast? Okay, I'll boast. I feel a little foolish, but here goes." As you read Paul's letter, you can almost picture these jealous rivals pulling out their check lists to see if he would measure up. But to their surprise, all he did was point to his suffering and weaknesses.

"You guys want to see what a big hit I've made? Here, let me list a few of my illustrious credentials. Let's see . . . I've been spit on. I've been beaten. Maybe you'd like to hear about how much time I've spent in jail. . . . Oh, yes, I've been shipwrecked, too. The Gentiles hate me. And the Jews—they can't stand me."

He went on to list more awards and honors. "You want to know what kind of grand entrances and exits I make? Well, I was lowered in a basket out of a side window one night. I would have used the door, but some guards were waiting there to arrest me."

The climax came when Paul started talking about his visions.

"Now I know you guys have visions every other day. Let me tell you about one of mine. But it wasn't yesterday—in fact, it must have been about fourteen years ago. It was pretty exciting up there in heaven. But you'll never catch me doing what you do—keeping people on the edge of their seats listening to all the details."

He went on. "But I *will* tell you *one* thing that happened. God was so impressed with my ability to handle all of this that He gave me something else along with my vision—a thorn in the flesh to keep me from becoming conceited!"

At this point the sarcasm stopped. Looking his opponents straight in the eye, as it were, he told them what his first reaction was to this new form of suffering God had sent him.

"Three times," he emphasized, "I pleaded with the Lord to take it from me. But He said to me, 'My grace is sufficient for you, *for my power is made perfect in weakness*'" (2 Cor. 12:8-9, italics mine).

Did you catch that? God answered Paul by saying, as the Living Bible puts it, "I am with you; that is all you need. My power shows up best in weak people."

If God's power shows up best in weak people, then why should we complain when we suffer and hurt? Instead, why not say with Paul:

> Therefore, I will boast all the more gladly about my weaknesses, so that Christ's power may rest on me. That is why, for Christ's sake, I delight in weakness, in insults, in hardships, in persecutions, in difficulties. For when I am weak, then I am strong (2 Cor. 12:9-10).

5 God's Showcase

Our God is a wonderful God. Just one good look at the miracle of childbirth, the beauty of nature, or the complexity of the solar system can tell us that. These awesome wonders give us a glimpse of how powerful, creative, and wise He is. But God has other qualities, too, virtues men would never see if suffering and sin didn't give them a chance to show themselves.

Take His kindness, for instance. Would we really appreciate the good health He gives if none of us were ever sick? Would God's forgiveness ever grip us if He never let us feel the piercing guilt of our sins? And what about His compassion in answering our prayers? How would we learn of it if we never had any needs to pray about? You see, the problems we face highlight the mercies of our God.

But not only that—our problems also provide a showcase for the good qualities that *people* have, too. Let me give you an example.

Picture a young man who is interested in a certain girl. He has been looking for a way to show her he likes her without being too obvious. One evening he is driving home from the office when whom should he spot but this very girl, stranded beside the road with a flat tire. Fantastic! Pulling his car onto the shoulder, he eases it up behind hers, flips on the emergency blinkers, and offers his assistance.

"That's sweet of you," she responds, "but please don't bother. You're wearing good clothes. I'll just call a garage."

"Forget it," he objects, searching her trunk for the jack. "We'll have you fixed up in no time."

A few minutes later it begins to rain. He insists she wait in his car where it's dry. After tightening the last bolt and banging on the hub cap, he joins her back in his car—dripping wet and with a bit of grease on his slacks. She apologizes for causing him such trouble, but he generously brushes aside any sympathy.

"C'mon," he says, starting the car, "we'll take this tire to a station and get it patched. I'd hate to see you get another flat and not have a spare. Your car will be all right here for a little while."

After a brief pause, trying his best to sound offhand, he adds, "Say, maybe while they're fixing it we could get a cup of coffee or something."

She smiles. "I'd like that."

There you have it. What could have been more right than for everything to go so wrong! Any other time, being late, having a flat, changing it in the rain, and soiling nice clothes would have been a frustrating nuisance. But here it gave the young man a chance to show sacrifice and kindness for the girl—something he desperately wanted to do. And it gave her the chance to feel special and cared for.

That's what problems do for us in life. Though bad in themselves, they allow people to show concern and other kindnesses to one another. Do you remember my sharing with you about the time I broke my nose after a tumble on an icy parking lot? Seeing me shivering with cold as I lay bleeding on that blacktop, everyone removed their coats and piled them on me for warmth. We call this selflessness, and it's something we all admire. But if I had had no need, if I had not been "suffering" at that moment, there would have been no chance for those around to demonstrate that selflessness.

Also, in order to be selfless at that point, each person offering a coat had to go cold for awhile. They needed to "suffer" in order to be kind to me. If each of them had been carrying five extra coats and had loaned one of them to keep me warm, it would have proved nothing. Able to stay warm themselves, it would have meant no real sacrifice on their part. But my suffering gave them a chance to share, and their sharing caused them to "suffer" in a small, yet real, way. Suffering was a necessary part of the selflessness shown that evening.

The same holds true for nearly every good thing a person can think or do. Suffering sets the stage on which good qualities can perform. If we never had to face fear, we would know nothing about courage. If we never had to weep, we would never know what it was like to have a friend wipe tears from our eyes.

But what does all of this have to do with God? When I say that suffering is able to bring out the best in us, am I singing some sort of hymn to human goodness? Not at all! By praising human goodness I'm actually praising God's goodness. For, you see, *God* is the author of every good and noble thing in the world (James 1:17). All of the love, kindness, sharing, and forgiveness that one person has ever shown to another comes ultimately from Him. We are made in His image—even those of us who don't acknowledge Him. Of course, that image is marred and tainted by sin. But it's still there, and whenever we do something good . . . we prove it!

Of all the suffering we might go through that helps us point people to God, there is one kind which seems to do it best. I am speaking of persecution. You have probably noticed how diamond arrangements in a jewelry store are usually set off with a dark, velvety cloth as a background. That is because the soft darkness of the cloth contrasts with, and enhances, the sharp lines and brightness of the gems. In the same way, when someone hurls abuse at a Christian's faith, that abuse acts as a velvety cloth. It makes the surprising love the Christian shows in return shine all the more brightly.

In the New Testament, Christians are told to love those who treat them badly. That's because our world is starving for the taste of genuine love. I'm not talking about soap-opera love where "I love you" usually means "I love me and want what you can give." I'm not even talking about "brotherly love." For "If you love those who love you, what credit is that to you? . . . Even 'sinners' do that" (Luke 6:32-33). What I *am* talking about is love that costs, love that gives until it hurts—even when it knows it won't get anything in return. In order for the world to see that kind of love, they need to see Christians who dare to follow Christ's example. And what was the example Christ set? He loved even those who flogged Him and beat Him.

> For what credit is it to bear it patiently, if you do wrong and are beaten for it? But if you do right and patiently suffer for it, it is pleasing in the sight of God. Indeed, it was to this kind of living that you were called, because Christ also suffered for you, leaving you an example that you might follow His footsteps. He never committed a sin, and deceit was never found on His lips. Although He was abused, He never retorted; although He continued to suffer, He never threatened, but committed His case to Him who

> judges justly. He bore our sins in His own body on the cross. . . . By His wounds you have been healed (1 Peter 2:20-24 WILLIAMS).

If Christ had not experienced real abuse, who would have seen His forgiveness? And if His punishment had been deserved, what would have been so special about the fact that He willingly submitted to it without fighting back? But as it is, His response to suffering gave the world a long, hard look at what God is like. And the result? Like Peter said, "By His wounds you have been healed!"

Some of you reading this book are Christians whose families, friends, neighbors, and business associates may not think much of what you believe. Perhaps they don't mind letting you know that either! Let me ask you something: Have you learned to view these pressures as God's answers to your prayers? Some hearts can only be melted by the warmth of real love. And the only way they'll experience that love is for someone to be nice to them in the face of their nastiness! If they treat you nicely, and you love them in return, so what? "Even 'sinners' do that." But if they treat you badly, what an opportunity! Then you can display the gem of Christlike forgiveness against the velvety cloth of suffering. God's greatness will be displayed from the platform of your problems.

* * * *

Over ten years ago my friend Diana walked into my hospital ward with her Bible and tried to explain to me the things I've shared with you in this chapter. But at the time I just couldn't believe God would stoop to give me a broken neck just so He could look good. That theory made it almost seem as if He were on some kind of an ego trip.

But think about that ego trip idea for a minute.

Suppose *you*—like God—were the most true, just, pure, lovely, and praiseworthy being in existence. And what if everything else in the universe that had any of these qualities got them from you? Because they reflected, to some extent, you? For that matter, suppose that without you these qualities would never have existed?

If that were the case, then for anyone around you to improve in any way, they would have to become more like you. For you to ask men to think about these good qualities would be to ask them to think about you. Their ego trips would be wrong, for then they would be centering their thoughts around sin and imperfection. But your ego trip would be glorious. Indeed, it would be the only hope for mankind, for your so-called ego trip would revolve around perfection.

So when God asks us to think about Him, He asks us to think about everything that is true, just, pure, lovely, and praiseworthy. This often requires suffering, and we think, "How awful." But actually His packages of suffering are wrapped with mercy, because He knows how desperately we need His qualities to become ours. For what if God did "leave us alone"? Suppose He never again sent any trials specifically intended to point us and others to Him. Would all suffering cease? Not on your life! It would only abandon us to a form of suffering far worse. Left to ourselves, with our sinful natures unchecked, in our greed and hate we would destroy one another.

But as it is, He screens the suffering, filtering it through fingers of love, giving us only that which works for good and which He knows will point us to Him. And He knows something else, too. He knows that if we come to know Him as Savior and Lord, we will eventually go to heaven where we will never suffer again.

6 When Nobody's Watching

You may have noticed that so far most everything I've said about our trials has to do with how our response to them affects other people. It's exciting to know that the way we handle our own problems can encourage others and move them to glorify God.

But that doesn't apply to some of you reading this book because you have little or no contact with other people. Perhaps you are an elderly person, living alone, who seldom gets out and has few visitors. Your active social life of yesteryear has been exchanged for a quieter sort of life—maybe reading, caring for a pet, or keeping up a small garden. "How can the sufferings I endure build up those around me?" you may be asking. "There isn't anybody around me!" How can your response to trials help God's cause when there is no one around to witness and consider?

Or how about those of you who rub shoulders with plenty of people all the time but have no real and intimate contact with them? Discussion about the weather, sports, and fashions may fill your day while the real issues of life, the kind that eat at you when you lie awake thinking at night, stay harbored deep inside. The mountains you face are unknown to those at work as you pass them in the hall with a smiling "Good morning." That's because there are some problems you just can't share with anyone and everyone. But then again, if people don't know about your problems, how can they benefit from watching you handle them?

Perhaps it is even more frustrating when the few people who do observe your godly response to suffering don't seem to be affected. Your example doesn't encourage them, and the sustaining grace of your God doesn't impress them. When that happens, you feel like a political candidate who has quit his job and spent thousands of dollars to campaign for office, only to lose the election. All of that suffering for nothing!

To suffer for nothing—what an awful thought. For our beliefs, yes. For our families, definitely. For things we want, perhaps. But for nothing? What a tragedy! It makes no difference whether we're actually alone or simply lonely—if we get the feeling that our pains and sorrows are worthless and unproductive, it can drive us to despair.

If there was any person I ever knew whose suffering seemed to be for nothing, it was Denise Walters. Those of you who read my first book will remember her as one of my four roommates in Greenoaks Rehabilitation Hospital, along with Betty Glover, B.J., and Ann. A year and a half before I arrived at Greenoaks, Denise was completing her senior year as a pretty and popular cheerleader at Western High School in Baltimore. One morning she stumbled as she and some schoolmates were bouncing up a flight of stairs between classes. No one thought much about it, and her friends helped brush off her clothes and retrieve her scattered books.

"Getting kind of clumsy in your old age, aren't you?" kidded one.

"I don't know what it was," answered Denise, tilting her head with a confused look. "My legs feel kind of weak."

"It's probably that slim-down diet you're always on," suggested her best friend. "Of all people, you sure don't need to lose any weight; you look great. You could afford to eat more than just a carrot and apple at lunch."

"I guess you're right," Denise agreed, and they all went on to class.

But by the end of the day she could hardly walk. Arriving home, she went straight to bed, and when she woke for dinner her legs were paralyzed. Within a short time her arms were paralyzed, and before long she was blind—the victim of an unusual and accelerated case of multiple sclerosis.

Lying motionless in her hospital bed at Greenoaks, Denise Walters knew what it meant to suffer. She couldn't watch TV. Neither could she gaze out the window. The only way she could enjoy a book was if someone took the time to sit and read it aloud to her. As for conversation, it took real effort to speak even a few sentences. Most difficult of all, she knew she was dying. Friends did occasionally drop by, but prolonged stays in a hospital eventually weed out all but the most committed visitors. In the end, it was mainly her mom, a wonderful Christian lady, who faithfully came every night to read the Bible and pray with her dying daughter who also loved Jesus.

The amazing thing about Denise was that she never complained. You might think this was the reason God let her suffer—so people could see her patience and be turned to Him. But that just didn't happen. In the first place, very few ever saw her. Her mom and roommates were about the only non-hospital people with whom she had any contact. And even we, her roommates, only brought up topics of conversation that were so shallow they never gave what was going on inside of Denise a chance to show. As far as she knew, nobody saw or cared about her love for God and her trust in His plan. Perhaps the saddest thing was that even on a rare day when a ray of that love and trust would manage to shine

through the dense fog of our spiritual blindness, it made no difference. Nobody ever told her, "I want the kind of life you have. How do I get it?" Her suffering seemed to be for nothing, like precious rainfall pattering down upon an unappreciative ocean while desert dwellers only miles away languish from thirst.

Five years after I left Greenoaks, Denise died. The news stirred mixed emotions in me. Of course, I was joyful that her pain was over and she was now with the Lord. But those long, trying, and seemingly wasted months prior to her death bothered me. I shared my uneasy feelings with Diana and Steve one night as we sat talking around the fireplace at my house. After a moment's thought, Diana was the first to speak.

"Judging from bits and pieces of things Denise said, I don't think she saw her situation as a waste," she began.

I agreed, but confessed I didn't understand why. "You knew the girls in that room, Di. You visited me often enough. Denise never got through to us."

"Maybe not," Diana replied. "But she knew you girls weren't the only ones around."

"You know what I mean, Di. Big deal. So a nurse stopped in every now and then. They were too busy rushing around to have anything Denise ever said or did rub off on them."

"I'm not talking about the nurses," Diana said, looking me right in the eye. "I'm talking about God and the whole spiritual world—you know, angels and demons. People might not have noticed, but they sure did."

Well, of course I knew God had been watching the whole time, though I'll admit it sometimes didn't feel that way. But angels and demons? I never realized they were watching, too.

Diana continued. "Jon, the Bible makes clear that the spiritual world is intensely concerned with the thoughts and affections of every human being. Why, the mind of the lowliest and most insignificant man is a battlefield where the mightiest forces of the universe meet in warfare."

Sensing that Diana was about to "wax eloquent" as she often does, I interrupted her before she got too far. "Diana, that sounds like something straight out of science fiction. Can you show me in the Bible where you get all this?"

Well, that was all the encouragement she needed. And so by the dim light of the fire and a single lamp, Diana and Steve took me through Scripture.

"Sure angels are interested in what men do," she related excitedly. Then leafing through her Bible like a tour guide who had been there before, she pointed out a verse to me. "Take a look at this." It was Luke 15:10.

"There is rejoicing in the presence of the angels of God over one sinner who repents," I read, half to myself, half mumbled aloud.

"Can you imagine?" she exclaimed. "It says there that God's angels actually get 'emotionally excited' when men choose to do what's right!"

"Do you think they're looking at us right now?" I asked, sneaking glances around the room, half-expecting to hear wings rustling behind the curtains.

"Sure," Steve spoke up. And taking Diana's Bible, he flipped over to Ephesians 3:10. "Here's another verse that proves the spiritual world has its eyes on us. Catch this—God uses the way He brings Christians together and works in their lives to teach the angels and demons about how wise and powerful He is."

"I get it!" I lit up. "We're kind of like a blackboard on which God draws lessons about Himself."

So her life wasn't a waste, I reasoned. *Denise knew that although not many people may have cared, someone* was *watching her in that lonely hospital room—a great many someones.*

Several years after this talk with Diana and Steve, I was speaking at a church one Sunday night in the Baltimore area. In my time of sharing I briefly mentioned Denise and her admirable faith during her illness. Two women came up to the platform after the meeting and explained that they worked with Denise's mother. They said they couldn't wait to get to work the following Monday morning and let Mrs. Walters know that I had spoken of her daughter.

This was tremendous! For a long time I had wanted to get in touch with Mrs. Walters to share with her the things Diana and Steve had shared with me from the Bible, but I hadn't known how to reach her.

"When you see her," I pleaded, "please give her a message from me. Please let her know that Denise's life was not in vain. I know it seems those eight long years in that lonely hospital bed didn't count for much or do anybody any good. But angels and demons stood amazed as they watched her uncomplaining and patient spirit rising as a sweet-smelling savor to God."

Maybe some of you are like Denise—alone . . . or just lonely. But next time you're tempted to think that your response to your trials is doing no one any good, before you give up the battle, turn to those verses my friends and I discussed that evening beside our fireplace. It might help remind you that sombody *is* watching. Somebody cares. You might even find yourself listening for the rustling of wings!

7 Breaks Us And Makes Us

Over the centuries God's promise in Romans 8:28 has been a Christian favorite. "Moreover we know that to those who love God, who are called according to his plan, everything that happens fits into a pattern for good" (PHILLIPS). In my first book I shared how I took the "good" toward which everything was working to mean I would regain the use of my limbs, go to college, get married, and have a family. But then a friend showed me the verse that followed, and it explained the real "good" that my trials were accomplishing. "For those God foreknew he also predestined *to be conformed to the likeness of his Son.*" The great Sculptor had taken in hand the hammer of suffering and was chiseling away at my character to shape it like Christ's.

I must admit that at first this whole idea of God giving me trials "for my good" and "to make me more like Christ" didn't excite me very much. I felt like a child who's about to be spanked listening to the old "This-is-going-to-hurt-me-more-than it's-going-to-hurt-you" speech. *Yeah, sure. Where does God get the nerve to claim that He let me break my neck because He loves me so much? Some kind of love!*

I remember coming across a book by C. S. Lewis called *The Problem of Pain* in which he dealt with that very problem—how could a loving God allow a world with so much pain and sickness? Everything he said was right on target, but one thing especially hit home. He explained that in accusing God of not being loving, many of us have taken just one aspect of love—kindness—and blown it up as if it were the whole thing. But what about the other aspects of love . . . like constructive criticism, or correction, or pushing a person to do his best? If by "love" we mean keeping another from all suffering or discomfort, then God is not always loving—and neither is a doctor who sticks a needle into the bottom of a crying infant.

Lewis went on to say that we as humans are most exacting and demanding on the people and things we care for and love the most. I knew he was right. As an artist, sketches I care little about I just leave alone, letting the mistakes go. But when I get excited about a drawing it gets "bruised and battered" with erasures and revisions. It seems God deals with us that way. For us to ask God to leave us alone and not refine us is to ask Him to love us less, not more!

> What would really satisfy us would be a God who said of anything we happened to like doing, "What does it matter so long as they are contented?" We want, in fact, not so much a Father in Heaven as a grandfather in Heaven—a senile ["old gentleman"] who, as they say, "liked to see young people enjoying themselves," and whose plan for the universe was simply that it might be truly said at the end of each day, "A good time was had by all."[3]

Okay. So God loves us. So His motive in suffering is to make us more like Christ. But how does suffering work? Is there some mystical link between problems and piety? Does being made helpless automatically make us holy? Of course, the answer is no. Just think about some of those prison cells that would be empty today if only the men and women who filled them had learned their lesson in their younger years. For some of them, the more knife fights they lost and the more often they landed in jail, the more calloused they became. Some people are like that: their trials harden them rather than teach them. But if the Holy Spirit has gotten your heart even slightly ready—well, as the old saying goes, "The same sun that hardens clay melts wax."

But how exactly does the wax melt? Is it just that trials make us go out and initiate a positive-thinking, I-can-do-it, self-help program? No. Of course, it is true that exercising our wills to try and follow Christ's example is an important part of becoming like Him. But even our best efforts fall so far short of His life that we look like a glove trying to imitate a human hand. As the glove needs the hand, so we need Christ Himself to live out His character in us. That's what the apostle Paul meant when he said, "It is *God* who is at work within you, giving you the will and the power to achieve his purpose" (Phil. 2:13 *Phillips*, italics mine). Now that we know who it is who makes us like Christ, let's find out how He does it.

Breaks Us

Before almost any good thing can be achieved in our lives, we need to be broken. This involves losing our pride, bowing our wills, and seeing our sinful selves for who we really are. Usually when we first enter God's family, we are full of brokenness. But like a poor man who stumbles upon sudden wealth, we soon forget the pit from which we were lifted. Bit by bit pride and self-sufficiency seep back into our lives and, unlike our first few weeks with Christ, "little" sins slip by unchecked and ignored.

To keep us from totally sliding back down the spiritual hill which we've started to climb, God chastens us. When He does, we may think it's because He's given up on us and wants to "trade us in on a newer model" which will give Him less trouble. But the fact that He disciplines us proves we are His very own children, for a parent doesn't spank a child who isn't his (Heb. 12:7-8). It also proves He loves us, for wise parents spank their children if they truly love them (Heb. 12:5-6). Someday when we stand before God's throne to receive our rewards for the lives we lived as Christians, imagine how glad we'll be that God didn't just let us get away with all our sinfulness while still on earth!

Now just as a mere stern glance from dad will send one child in a family running in tears to his room, while with another child dad must use a belt, so God must use different means to produce brokenness in His various children. Sometimes the mere pangs of a guilty conscience are enough to bring us low—hearing a convicting sermon or feeling our mediocrity in comparison with the life of a great Christian we've been reading about. Other times it may take a broken arm, financial pressure, or embarrassment.

Whatever the method, when the crunch first comes we may stubbornly think to ourselves, "I can handle this. Nobody's going to get me to bend." But as God continues to forcefully press, we begin to realize that we can't handle it, that there is no good thing within us, and that He intends to root out all of ugly Self and replace it with His character. But remember, replacing our sin with His righteous character doesn't make us robots or less than ourselves; it frees us to be all that we were really meant to be.

It took a broken neck to back me into a corner and get me thinking seriously about the lordship of Christ. But, like everyone else, I still need refining.

Having to wait for someone when I'm thirsty for a glass of water, or wetting a friend's car seat when my leg bag springs a leak are two of the methods God sometimes uses to keep me in spiritual shape. But very often His tool will be a guilty conscience, one of the more effective weapons in God's arsenal of suffering.

God used this weapon on me one night about a year ago as I lay in bed talking with my sister Jay. We were commenting about how her daughter Kay was growing up to become quite a young lady for a twelve-year-old and how excited we were that she was attending a Christian school and growing in the Lord. That led us to think about the spiritual condition of our neighbor Kathy, Kay's best friend. Kathy was always popping in and out of our house—bubbly, enthusiastic, a cute girl like Kay. We had never really talked to Kathy about the Lord since it was hard to catch her either alone or sitting still! So one evening, a few weeks before, we had invited her down to watch Billy Graham on television. As we all sat around the living room eating pretzels and watching, Kathy had really listened. After the message she said to no one in particular, "Boy, if I was in that arena I'd go forward." Jay and I caught each other's eye, but before we had a chance to talk with her she had to go home.

I knew I should be the one to follow up on that evening because if she'd listen to anybody, she'd surely listen to me. Kay had told me that Kathy had read my book, and I knew she liked me. She was always quick to get me a glass of water and do little things for me. She had even confided to my sister Jay that she thought I was one of the neatest people in the world. But the next day Kathy had to visit with her relatives. The day after, I was busy with something else, and as the month wore on I didn't seem to have the chance to talk with her. My mind was filled with all the speaking responsibilities I had in the coming weeks, and Kathy got placed on the back shelf.

Well, on the evening I lay talking with Jay, I had just gotten back from one of those speaking trips. I was tired in body and mind and felt like relaxing and not discussing anything heavy. But coming out of the bathroom still combing her hair, Jay asked me in all innocence if I'd ever talked to Kathy about the Lord.

"No, I haven't talked to Kathy about the Lord," I mumbled as I tried to shut her out and continued staring at the late news on TV. But a slight stab of conscience wouldn't let me pay attention to what was on the screen.

To shift the blame, a minute later I let drop, "Why haven't you talked to her?"

"Come on, Joni" Jay replied, "you're closer to Kathy than I am. And besides, you know how much she looks up to you."

By this time my pride was beginning to hurt, my defenses were up, and I quickly got stubborn. "I just haven't had time," I snapped.

"Whoa!" Jay exclaimed. "You have time to fly all over the country giving out the gospel, but no time for your niece's best friend?"

Well, that did it. "How come everybody thinks I'm supposed to be Miss Win-the-World all the time?" I sputtered in pride and anger, and then went on to huff and puff in my defense.

But as soon as I had finished my "speech," the arrow of conscience struck my heart. Not being able to get up and leave the room, I slammed my eyes shut and turned my face away to bury it in the pillow. Inside, my heart was burning as hot as the tears which stained my cheeks. I hated to admit it, but I knew Jay was right.

After the lights in the room were out for the night, a small projector inside my head began to run mental movies of all the time Kathy and I had spent together when she was adjusting my drawing easel, emptying my leg bag, or giggling to me about her boyfriends. There were plenty of times I could've talked more seriously with her. Needless to say, my spirit was crushed and my pride was broken. More than that, I got a full glimpse of how wretched I was in the light of God's glory.

God must really be angry with me right now, I thought to myself. But as I churned that idea over in my mind, I knew it wasn't true. The verse in Ephesians popped into my mind—where we're told not to *grieve* the Spirit of God (Eph. 4:30). *I guess that's it. He's not angry with me; "hurt" is more the word.*

I remembered a sermon I had heard once on just how thoroughly Christ dealt with our sins at His death. "When Jesus was sweating and suffering on that dreadful cross outside the walls of Jerusalem," the pastor had said, "it was as if God accused Him with flaming eyes: 'Jesus, why did You tell that lie? Why did You hate Your neighbor? Why did You cheat, lust, and covet? I am punishing You here for all these things!' Of course, Christ had never done one of them, but we had, and every single one of your sins and mine was put on His account there."

I remembered how unjust it had seemed for Christ to be treated so. The preacher continued: "Suffering as though our sins were His own, He underwent the indescribable horror of having to cry, 'My God, my God, why hast Thou forsaken me?' And do you know why? On that day God forsook His own Son so that our sins could be totally erased and, in contrast, He could say to us, 'I will *never* leave you or forsake you.' If you have made Jesus Christ your Lord and Savior, dear friend, all God's anger for your sins has been poured out on Christ; He has none left for you."

No anger left for me! It made me feel so ashamed I could hardly stand it. The goodness of God was, indeed, leading me to repentance (Rom. 2:4). *God,* I breathed silently, *here I am flying all over the place to tell people about You, and yet I've never really talked to my next-door neighbor, Kathy. Oh, please forgive me for being so blind and for hurting You so. Forgive me for putting my own convenience above the value of Kathy's salvation. And thank You for loving a vermin like me.*

In case you're wondering, I imagine a vermin to be any disgusting little creature that slithers along the ground, eats dirt, and deserves to be stepped on! David had the same feeling when he said in Psalm 22 that he was no man but a worm. Unlike a snake that will rear up its head and hiss and strike back, worms can't defend themselves. They know who they are and that they're about to be crushed. I felt that way that night. I understood there was no good thing within me. I was a broken person, and that's right where God wanted me.

Little did I realize it, but in making me broken, God was making me more like Christ, for Christ Himself was the prime example of a broken man. Not that Jesus ever had a stubborn, sinful character in need of remodeling. Nothing of the sort. But in leaving heaven's glories to become a man, He demonstrated the kind of submission to the Father that we can have only by becoming broken. In fact, that's what brokenness is all about—realizing what little right we have to run our own lives and, therefore, submitting ourselves to God.

Our attitude should be the same as that of Jesus Christ:

> Who, being in very nature God,
> did not consider equality with God
> something to be grasped,

> but *made himself nothing,* taking the very
> nature of a servant,
> being made in human likeness.
> And being found in appearance as a man, he
> *humbled himself*
> and *became obedient* to death—
> even death on a cross!
> (Phil. 2:5-8, italics mine).

What character Christ has!

Andrew Murray once mentioned that as water seeks to find the lowest level and fill it, so God seeks to fill us with the character of His Son when we are emptied, broken and low. When you think about it, that in itself is enough to give us real hope that even our most difficult sufferings are worth it.

Speaking of being filled, how filled I was with a godly joy and excitement as Kathy and Kay came bounding into my bedroom the next morning. I don't think I've ever been so glad to see someone in my life. After talking with Kathy about the Lord for only a few minutes, it was obvious the Holy Spirit had already done His work as the "advance man," softening her heart and opening her mind.

As we bowed our heads and she prayed in simple words for Christ to come into her life as Savior and Lord, I couldn't resist the urge to peek up at her for a moment. *You know, God,* I smiled inside, *being broken hurts for a while, but it sure is worth it in the end.*

> No discipline seems pleasant at the time, but painful. Later on, however, it produces a harvest of righteousness and peace for those who have been trained by it. (Heb. 12:11).

Gets Our Minds on Spiritual Things

Chastening is valuable, but there are other, more positive, ways God uses suffering to make us like Christ. For instance, take the way a good father deals

with his nine-year-old son. Of course, whenever the son gets out of line and disobeys, dad disciplines him. But even when he's good his father assigns him certain tasks that often, to a nine-year-old, seem like punishment and are just as unpleasant. Maybe his job is to take out the garbage twice a week or cut the grass; perhaps he has to put part of his allowance into the bank. Whatever, the boy might think to himself, "Just because dad has to work all day he doesn't want me to have any fun either." But that's not it at all. The wise father is training his son to be responsible so that when he grows up he'll be ready to face the world.

At times we are like the nine-year-old boy. We imagine God is making us suffer because "He doesn't want us having any fun," when what He's really doing is getting minds off the toys and games of this world. Colossians 3:1-4 talks about this when it says we are not to set our affections on the passing things of this earth, but are to set them on heavenly glories above where Christ is seated at the right hand of God.

When I was on my feet, I found it extremely difficult to set my affections in heaven. I was far too interested in the glittering things of now, caught up with dating the right guy, driving the right car, getting into the right college, and being seen with the right crowd. But when it finally hit me that I would never again walk, dance, swim, ride, play guitar, drive a car, or score a lacrosse goal, I was *driven* to start thinking about heaven. Not because heaven suddenly became an escape or some sort of psychological cop-out. But because I began to realize that my only true hope for any permanent happiness lay there. Suddenly, Bible passages about God's purposes in suffering that had seemed so boring before held my attention; I read with greater interest than a stockbroker reads the Dow-Jones averages.

By now, living each day in the light of eternity has become such a way of life for me that I almost forget what the old way of living and thinking was like. But God gave me a reminding glimpse not long ago.

A group of friends had come over to our farm that evening, and while my sister's husband picked his guitar we all sat around talking, laughing and singing by the light of the crackling fire in the huge fieldstone fireplace. Our rustic living room is well over 150 years old, a converted slaves' quarters with ceiling beams my dad put in from an old clipper ship and two-feet-thick plastered walls spotted with dad's rugged paintings of scenes from the old West. The handwoven Indian blanket hanging opposite the driftwood which stands guard over the mantle gives the final touch of atmosphere to this cozy hideaway.

Because I feel comfortable in my wheelchair, usually I just stay in it while others settle themselves onto the couch or in an easy chair or perhaps down on the rug with their backs against the wall. But tonight one of the guys had seated me on the couch beside my friend Betsy. After she had crossed my legs for me, I looked so "normal" that, except for my arm braces, anyone coming in who didn't know me would never know I was paralyzed.

For a while I just sat back and took in everything going on in the room—laughing and clapping and singing. Then Betsy turned to me and asked how I felt being on the couch.

"You know what's really interesting?" I answered, thoughtfully scanning the room again and then glancing over at her. "In the short time I've been in this position on the couch, maybe forty-five minutes, I can see how easy it would be for me to forget God if I were on my feet."

You see, sitting on that couch looking very unparalyzed had made it easier for me to imagine myself doing things like getting my own glass of Coke out of the fridge, putting on a record, answering the door, or any number of things a normal person can do. I could also see how easy it would be, for me at least to again become so wrapped up in the little things of "now" that God would soon get only a token of my thoughts.

When you think about it, a lot of us would never have thought about God in the first place had He not used some problems to get our attention. "God whispers to us in our pleasures, speaks in our consciences, but shouts in our pains: it is His megaphone to rouse a deaf world."[4] We would have gone comfortably right through our lives, scarcely giving Him or our eternal destiny a passing thought—until we got there. And so God mercifully puts pain and suffering in front of us as "blockades on the road to Hell."[5]

Paul and Timothy once mentioned that God had sent them some extremely difficult trials just so they would not rely on themselves but on God (2 Cor. 1:8-9). I could relate to those verses that evening. My chair, because it is visible, is a constant reminder of how much I depend upon Him. A sudden pain inside my back, a corset that breaks, or a battle with bedsores—all remind me how disabled I really am. They are the special marks of God's ownership of me. They get my thoughts and hopes on heaven. They make me more like Christ.

Do you like to have your cake and eat it, too? I sometimes do, and I'm probably not alone. Like the man who enjoys the weather of Florida but has a terrific job offer in New England, all of us are at some time faced with the crisis of having to decide between two worlds when we would dearly love to live in both.

There is no one who can appreciate this difficulty of deciding between two opposing desires more than the believer in Christ. On the one hand, the Holy Spirit helps him to love God and desire what is right. But on the other hand, his Christian commitment is constantly challenged by the lure of his own sinful nature. He would love to live in both worlds, but he must decide.

When it comes to the "big" sins like murder, drunkenness, or adultery, many of us have no trouble deciding to obey Christ. But it's the so-called "little" sins we try to hang onto, sins like worrying, complaining, or bitterness, that keep us with one foot in the kingdom and one foot in the world. Because these sins aren't as obvious as others, we would probably never really deal with them if God didn't force us. But since "little" sins are big to God, He does force us, and the method He uses is—you guessed it—suffering.

As you might imagine, worrying, complaining, and bitterness were often temptations to me as I struggled with the meaning of my paralysis in my early hospital days. Deep inside I knew they were wrong. But in my mind I justified myself by saying, "Surely God won't mind if I let off a little steam every now and then. I mean, after all, I *am* paralyzed!"

To make things worse, several months into my hospital stay I learned that I had to have an operation on the lower tip of my spine. The bone had been protruding through the skin and needed to be shaved. After the surgery I was forced to lay face down in my Stryker Frame for fifteen days while the stitches healed. Unless you've experienced it, you can't imagine what it feels like to be strapped in that awful canvas sandwich, face fitted into an opening that allows you to see only what's straight ahead. And in my case, that was the floor. *Boy, it's not enough that I've got to live life from a wheelchair; now I'm strapped on this torture rack counting tiles on the floor and can't move anything at all!*

If God had let me get away with this I would have been the loser—digging myself ever deeper into that miry pit. Nor would I have been of much use to Him. So what did God do? He added still another problem! During the first day of my two-week career as a slab of baloney in a canvas sandwich, He "mayonnaised" me with the Hong Kong flu! Suddenly, not being able to move was peanuts compared to not being able to breath comfortably. And those pounding headaches!

Why? I complained angrily. *Haven't I had enough?* But as I thought about it, I knew why. God was forcing me to open my eyes to what I was doing. No longer was my bitterness a tiny trickle; it was a raging torrent that could not be ignored. It was as if He were holding my anger up before my face and saying lovingly but firmly, "Stop turning your head and looking the other way. See! This is what you're doing. It's a sin. What are you going to do about it?" He was forcing me to make a decision.

At that point, God had me backed into a corner, the kind of corner we all need to be backed into sometimes. I had to face the facts and make a decision: Was I going to follow Christ in this thing or not? The pressure had gotten so strong that I was either going to have to give the situation over to Him completely or allow myself the short-lived luxury of totally wallowing in anger and bitterness. Either route would give some immediate sense of release, but they were two different medicines which couldn't be mixed. There could no longer be any middle ground.

When I was faced with that kind of ultimatum, it helped me see clearly what an evil, wicked course the alternative to following Him was. I came to realize that *if I was to be a true disciple of Christ, it was going to cost me my sins*. Were they worth more to me than my fellowship with God? *Of course not*, I decided, and breathed a prayer of repentance toward God. And as the steamy vapors rising from the hot basin beneath the frame cleared my head, I knew in my heart that my obedience to God was rising as a sweet-smelling vapor to Him.

When God brings suffering into your life as a Christian, be it mild or drastic, He is forcing you to decide on issues you have been avoiding. He is pressing you to ask yourself some questions: Am I going to continue trying to live in two worlds, obeying Christ and my own sinful desires? Or am I going to refuse to worry? Am I going to be grateful in trials? Am I going to abandon my sins? In short, am I going to be like Christ?

He provides the suffering, but the choice is yours.

When God wants to drill a man,
And thrill a man, and skill a man,
When God wants to mold a man
To play the noblest part,
When He yearns with all His heart
To build so great and bold a man
That all the world shall be amazed,
Then watch His methods, watch His ways!
How He ruthlessly perfects
Whom He royally elects;
How He hammers him and hurts him,
And with mighty blows converts him
Into shapes and forms of clay
Which only God can understand
While man's tortured heart is crying
And he lifts beseeching hands . . .
Yet God bends but never breaks
When man's good He undertakes;
How He uses whom He chooses,
And with mighty power infuses him,
With every act induces him to try
His splendor out,
God knows what He's about!

WHILE WE'RE WORKING ON THE PUZZLE

8 Trust And Obey

One of the special joys I remember about being on my feet was horseback riding. And what made riding so special was Augie, an old sorrel thoroughbred who knew everything there was to know about jumping. Now Augie certainly didn't look like a Class A thoroughbred. His long legs and thin body resembled the frame of an adolescent boy whose weight hadn't yet caught up with his height. That, coupled with his large head and Roman nose, made him too ugly a candidate to ever win any beauty contest. But he certainly knew how to jump fences, and at just about every horse show we would enter, Augie came away with the blue ribbons in all the open jumping classes.

In addition to the marvelous way he could pace himself, the exciting thing about Augie was the instant obedience and absolute trust he showed toward me. Whenever we entered a show ring he would quietly dance and prance in one place, never pulling on the reins, ears flicking backward and forward in anticipation of my command. I never had to tug his head; I just held his snaffel bit firmly against his mouth, keeping the reins low and taut. Whenever I wanted him to move ahead, all it took was a slight tightening of my knees against him and—flash! Off he would go!

Augie would confidently canter to the first jump, fly swiftly over it, and then flick his ears again, awaiting my directions for the next move. Over the second fence he would fly, then the third, fourth, and fifth, leaping through a complex maze of fences. Almost never did he shy away from a jump at the last second. After we would finish, Augie would be hot and lathered, and I often felt as I patted his shoulder that he was as pleased with his performance as I was.

Maneuvering a complicated jump pattern requires

a trusting and obedient horse. After completing a fence, the rider has to pull the horse up so he won't tire himself and so he can properly pace himself for the next fence. If the horse doesn't listen, they're both in trouble! Feeling the horse begin to shift his weight a few feet from the fence, the rider must know when to release the reins and give the horse his head so he'll be able to jump cleanly and clearly. The horse must trust his rider to do this. It's a two-way street; there must be real cooperation.

Augie and I had that kind of relationship. I knew his trust in me was absolute and complete. At my command he was eager to obey in an instant. It was the joy of Augie's great heart to do my will. It did not matter whether or not he understood the course of jumps before him. He showed no concern over how hard those four-foot rail jumps or five-foot triple spread jumps appeared. He simply loved to jump. And because he trusted my judgment, he loved to do my will.

For us humans, the path of life set before us often seems like a confusing maze of difficult, and sometimes painful, fences we are expected to hurdle. The more perplexing the pattern grows and the more demanding the discipline becomes, the more we are tempted to doubt the wisdom of our Rider. We feel like disobeying by balking at the jumps and avoiding the course.

The apostle Peter knew about this when he wrote his first epistle. His readers lived during the reign of the madman Nero and knew what it was like to have the threat of a torturous death hanging daily over their heads. Of course, Peter assured them that a great reward awaited them in heaven. But what were they to do in the meantime? How were they to respond *now* to the overwhelming and perplexing course before them? Peter advised them this way:

"So then, those who suffer according to God's will should commit themselves to their faithful Creator and continue to do good" (1 Peter 4:19).

Committing ourselves to our faithful Creator—that's *trusting* God. Continuing to do good—that's *obeying* Him. If you grew up attending church, you've probably sung that old hymn "Trust and Obey" many, many times. According to Peter, we couldn't find a better summary of what God expects of us when the hurdles are difficult and the pattern doesn't seem to make sense.

Trusting God

When you think about it, Augie's response to me didn't hinge on his approval of the course set before him. As a matter of fact, he didn't know or understand what was set before him. What counted was that he knew me. For years I had fed him, brushed him down, given him exercise, and led him to shelter away from the cold. We had built a relationship, and I had proven myself to him over and over again. By demonstrating myself trustworthy, I was able to so win Augie's confidence that he followed me in whatever I asked.

That same type of relationship built on trust was the key factor in saving our horses' lives several years ago. During the incident I mentioned earlier when someone set fire to my father's barn, our first thought was for the safety of the horses. Since fire can cause an otherwise calm horse to go wild with fear, we covered their eyes with blankets before leading them past the roaring flames and out to safety. Such an ordeal must be an unsettling thing for a horse. With so much noise and commotion surrounding him and the strange smell of smoke clogging his nostrils, one would imagine that then, of all times, a horse would desire the full use of his senses and faculties. But

Diana Mood (partner in JONI PTL) and Betsy Sandbower (right) help Joni plan her schedule

Joni's sister Kathy enjoys a typical Eareckson pastime—horseback riding

Niece Kay (right) with friend and neighbor, Kathy Mettee

Joni's parents, John and Lindy Eareckson

A special headset enables Joni to use the phone

On speaking tour in 1977 with Sheryl Bond and sister Jay (right)

Joni at the desk in her studio where she works, draws, and reads

Steve and Verna Estes and Joni work on *A Step Further*

here these humans were covering his eyes with a blanket that ordinarily went on his back and asking him to follow them when he could not even see. To the horse, in the words of C. S. Lewis, "the whole proceeding would seem, if it were a theologian, to cast grave doubts on the 'goodness' of man."[6] But fortunately our horses weren't theologians; they were horses. In that confusing moment when they could not understand, they trusted us to care for them as we had always done. There was no rebelling, no challenging of our wisdom or authority, and as a result we were able to save their lives.

How unlike these simple animals we are! They put tremendous confidence in their masters, mere human beings, yet the great God who has chosen to save and redeem us at such a precious price does not have our trust. "An ox knows its owner, and a donkey its master's manger, but Israel does not know, My people do not understand," marveled the Lord in Isaiah 1:3.

What causes this senseless lack of faith? It is our failure to realize just how much God has already done to prove Himself to us. We really don't know who our God is and what He is like. The men and women of the Bible considered God's character and nature to be the rock foundation on which their faith rested. "This I recall to my mind, therefore, I have hope," Jeremiah reminded himself amid the horror and confusion of the Babylonian invasion of Israel. "The Lord's lovingkindnesses indeed never cease, for His compassions never fail. They are new every morning; great is Thy faithfulness. . . . Therefore, I have hope in Him. The Lord is good to those who wait for Him" (Lam. 3:21-25). Jeremiah chose to depend on what He knew to be true about God from the Bible and from history instead of relying on his own assessment of things.

The apostle Paul's confidence during trials was not

based on the assumption that he could say, "I know why this is happening to me." Rather, it rested on the fact that he was able to say, "I know whom I have believed" (2 Tim. 1:12). The God he trusted was the One who, by His own power, had set the sun, moon, and stars in motion. It was He who, in infinite wisdom, had ladled out the sea, dreamed up space and time, formed the mountains, carved out rivers, scattered rain and hail, and conceived in His mind our very existence. But for Paul, the supreme demonstration of the wonderful nature and character of this great God was when He laid aside His divine splendor, took upon Himself the form of a servant, and died a martyr's death for us. "He who did not spare his own Son, but gave him up for us all—how will he not also, along with him, graciously give us all things?" (Rom. 8:32).

If God has done *that*, surely He has proved His intentions! When He covers our eyes with the blanket of a limited understanding, surely He deserves to be given "the benefit of the doubt," to put it mildly. He is worthy of our trust.

> The Hands that shaped the flaming spheres
> and set them spinning, vast light-years
>   away from Planet Earth,
> have laid aside the Robes of State,
> donned human likeness by the great
>   indignity of birth.
>
> The Hands, responsive to Love's Plan,
> that formed the God-reflector, Man,
>   of dust and destiny,
> outstretched—by Man's fierce hate impaled—
> wrought life anew, Love's Plan unveiled
>   upon Golgotha's Tree.
>
> The Hands that found it nothing strange
> to pucker up a mountain range
>   or ladle out a sea,

that balance Nature's systems still,
and shape all History to His will,
hold, and are molding, *me!*
—Marion Donaldson

What Is Trust?

When I speak of having faith in God during our times of suffering and crises, I am not talking about an emotion. Trusting God is not necessarily having trustful feelings. It is an act of the will. *Because essentially, trusting God is reasoning with yourself to act upon what you know in your head to be true, even though you do not feel like it is true.*

In those first months after my injury, the promises of God seemed anything but true. To my way of thinking, God was insane. How could this crazy paralysis possibly fit into a pattern of good for my life? I felt as though the despair of my soul was as bleak as the gray hospital walls which surrounded me. Even after I was able to return home, trusting the Lord seemed impossible. How could I be expected to believe when everything inside and outside of me screamed just the opposite?

The answer came on one of those long and pleasant evenings when Steve, Diana, and I were sitting around my parents' living room fireplace discussing spiritual things. Steve had his Bible and was explaining a passage he had just studied that week. Opening to chapter twenty of John's Gospel, he began reading where it described the disciples several days after Jesus' burial, hiding from the Jews in fear behind locked doors. Suddenly, Jesus appeared in the middle of the room and assured the astonished men that He had indeed risen.

For some reason Thomas was out when it all took place, and upon returning to the room later, he failed to find the excited report of his fellow disciples convincing. "Unless I see the scars in His hands and side, I will not believe it," he protested.

One week later in the same house, with the doors locked, Jesus appeared again to the huddled group. This time Thomas was there. The Lord addressed him, "Come here, Thomas. See My hands for yourself; touch My side. Stop doubting and believe."

Faced with the visible evidence, the only response the amazed disciple could give was the confession of worship, "My Lord and my God!"

Steve leaned forward just a bit more to add intensity and then read slowly from verse twenty-nine, directing its content right at me. "Then Jesus told him, 'Because you have seen me, you have believed; *blessed are those who have not seen and yet have believed*'" (italics mine).

The verse hit me with the force of a truck. Jesus wanted me to believe what He said without having to have tangible or visible proof. Sure, He could appear visibly right in my room. That would make believing so easy. But He wanted me to take Him at His word. Didn't I like to be taken at my word? Hadn't it felt good when the local store clerk would let me off if I was a few nickels short, saying, "Pay me next time. I know you're good for the money"? Didn't Jesus want to be treated the same way?

It took some gut effort, but from that time on whenever I had doubts, I reasoned to myself from the things I knew in Scripture about God's trustworthy nature. And I still have to do that sometimes. Feelings or no feelings, I cling to Jesus' words that in heaven I will be rewarded, not because I have seen and believed, but because not seeing, not feeling, I have *still* believed. By taking God at His word, sight unseen, you and I have the privilege of honoring God and of being commended in a way the twelve disciples never could be.

Obeying God

When God allows us to suffer, sometimes our tendency is to use our very trials as an excuse for sinning. We feel that since we've given God a little extra recently by taking such abuse, He owes us "a day off" when we can do as we please. This is a continual inner battle for me. I'll be sitting out on our porch on a beautiful spring day when suddenly the reality of my confinement will hit me hard. A little lustful fantasizing is sure inviting then, or maybe a few minutes of bitterness and self-pity. And it is so easy to justify. *Don't I already have to give up more than a lot of Christians just by being crippled?* I say to myself. *Doesn't my wheelchair entitle me to a little slacking off now and then?*

When we feel like this, if we sit down and examine our lame protests in the light of the Bible, they will vanish one by one. I have discovered in the Bible at least three good reasons why suffering does not give me any excuse to sin.

First, *God has promised that He provides for me, and for every other Christian, the desire and power to do what's right—no matter what the circumstances!* I used to think my trials were an exception—that He couldn't expect from me what He did from others because it was "a different story" in my case. But 1 Corinthians 10:13 told me, "No temptation has seized you except what is common to man."

It always seemed to me as I lay in my hospital bed that God was putting me through more than I could take. But 1 Corinthians 10:13 told me, "God is faithful; he will not let you be tempted beyond what you can bear."

Sometimes when lust and bitterness would lure me, I reasoned within myself, "There is no way I can say 'No' to bitterness and break free of sin's clutches this time." But, again, 1 Corinthians 10:13 told me,

"When you are tempted, he will also provide a way out so that you can stand up under it."

Now either I was right or He was right. Faced with a choice like that, I knew I just couldn't call God a liar. So when I sin during my sufferings, it's not because I have to. It's because I want to. God gives me grace to live in a wheelchair which He doesn't give you if you can walk; but He gives you grace to endure the death of a husband, the loss of your hearing, the plight of poverty, or whatever, which He doesn't give me. Each of us needs to use the grace God gives and to bear up faithfully under our own unique burdens.

Now that I knew I *could* obey, the question to be answered was—*would* I? This brought up the whole issue of the lordship of Christ—the second reason why I have no excuse to sin. *Before any of us ever "sign up" to follow Christ, He makes it clear that He is to be the Master and that following Him will require some real hardships for us.* There is no fine print in the contract. What we are getting into is plainly spelled out in His Word from the beginning—"If anyone would come after me, he must deny himself and take up his cross and follow me," He tells us. "No one who puts his hand to the plow and looks back is fit for service in the kingdom of God" (Mark 8:34; Luke 9:62).

Besides all of this, it is absurd to use suffering as a reason for sinning, when *suffering's very purpose is to turn us from our sin and make us like Christ.* Peter said that the person "who has suffered in his body is done with sin. As a result, he does not live the rest of his earthly life for evil human desires, but rather for the will of God" (1 Peter 4:1-2). During my stay in the hospital I met many people who wouldn't have given God the time of day when they were healthy. But a good splash of ice-cold suffering sure woke them out of their spiritual slumber. How silly to use something that was meant to wake us up as an excuse to doze off spiritually.

But wiping out my excuses for disobeying God wasn't all that the Bible did for me. It also gave me some exciting positive incentives *to* obey. Like joy, for instance. What gives more heartfelt joy than having a clear conscience, knowing that you haven't brought on your own troubles? And even when those troubles are your fault, by starting to obey again, you know that you've taken the first step in getting out from under the rod of correction. To top it all off, we know that "Blessed is the man who perseveres under trial, because when he has stood the test, he will receive the victor's crown" (James 1:12).

One final thought. Obeying God's command to love others is one of the most difficult things we ever have to do while suffering. Our own needs, pains, and griefs scream for our undivided attention. Yet giving in would do nothing but hurt us, for often healing only comes when we get our minds off ourselves and show concern for others and their cares and interests.

Recently, at a wedding shower for my friend Sheryl, I was having anything but a good day. My back ached, my corset was too tight, and the two got together and made my head throb. I've got to admit that my conscience wasn't treating me all that nicely either. It kept reminding me of a few things I'd said to a member of my family that morning, even though I had confessed those things to God. And looking around at all those smiling faces didn't help things much. *I should be happy today. After all, Sheryl's one of my best friends, and this is her special day!* About all I could do was work up a polite smile and hope nobody would corner me in conversation.

Staring blankly ahead, I was looking at, but not

really noticing, Pop Bond—Sheryl's father-in-law-to-be, the only man at the shower. Oblivious to the girlish chatter, Mr. Bond was picking his way around boxes and presents, snapping photos from this angle and that. But when he began to zoom his lens in on me, he stopped being a blur in my vision and suddenly came into focus.

"Oh, no," I protested. "Please, not me."

"Why not?" he said with a smile, and began walking toward me. "You look very pretty today."

My gaze dropped. "Well, Pop, I don't feel very pretty."

"That's no problem. This camera can make you look great even on a bad day," he joked, taking a seat on the folding chair beside me. "Here, let me show you this new lens I just bought."

With that, he opened his leather case and began displaying proudly, one by one, his host of camera attachments, explaining as he went.

"Now, just take a look at this new two-hundred-millimeter zoom lens. Why, you can focus and zoom with just one hand."

I have to admit, I wasn't very interested in hearing about his camera gismos. But I listened as this white-haired gentleman with the sparkling blue eyes continued. He told me how excited he was about his basement darkroom. Pride beamed in his eyes as he described the local awards some of his pictures had won.

"Um hum," I nodded casually, still not particularly impressed. But he did begin catching my ear when he started recounting a recent trip he had taken to Sagamore Horse Farm to photograph some of their breeding barns and springhouses. He went on to explain how he had returned to the farm weeks later to give the manager some of the finished photos he had taken there.

Pop really does love his hobby, I thought. *I admire that.* His story continued.

"The manager liked those shots so much, he asked if I'd come back and take pictures of their stallions," he exclaimed.

"No kidding!" I lit up a bit. "How did you get high-spirited thoroughbreds to stand still for a snapshot?"

"Well, it wasn't easy," he laughed and lifted a finger. "But we all got together and . . . ."

Before long, I began to realize I was interested in what Pop was saying and was really listening to him.

"Well, Pop," I smiled, "you'll just have to come up to our farm soon. Bring your cameras, and we'll make a day of it."

By the time the shower was over, I had discovered how much I really did care about this dear old gentleman and his hobby. More than that, I had genuinely forgotten all about my aches and pains and guilty conscience. The concern I had shown for him was the very remedy that worked wonders for me!

When God tells us to obey Him in our trials by putting others first, He knows what He's doing. He knows we won't be sorry.

Give, and it will be given to you. A good measure, pressed down, shaken together and running over, will be poured into your lap.
For with the measure you use, it will be measured to you (Luke 6:38).

9 Don't Compare ...Share!

As my bare feet positioned themselves on the edge of the wooden raft on that hot July afternoon in 1967, it never occurred to me that the murky Chesapeake Bay into which I was about to plunge concealed a shallow bottom. I should have known better, should have checked the depth. But the innocent-looking waters lured me into a trap which broke my neck and cost me the use of my hands and legs for the rest of my life.

There is an innocent-looking trap awaiting each person who suffers. It isn't a body of water, but an attitude. I am talking about the temptation to compare ourselves with others who seem to have it easier than we do. Just a few indulging dives into this perilous frame of mind, and we will find ourselves caught in a net of self-pity that robs our joy and dishonors God.

I was ensnared in this net during the early years of my paralysis. It's confining power particularly showed itself whenever I went shopping for clothes with my close friend Sheryl. Sheryl's clothes always fit her so well. In comparison, it seemed to me that mine hung on me like a sack. Watching her model an outfit for size made my face flush with envy, although I never told her.

"What do you think, Joni?" she would ask about a pants suit we were considering, turning first this way, then that, to see in the mirror from every angle.

"Looks great, Sheryl," I would answer, trying to sound excited in order to hide my jealousy. But inside I was burning. As she wheeled me up to the mirror so I could model the same outfit, all I could think of was, *God, how come I can't look like her? I can't even compare myself to a mannequin and come out winning—clothes fit them great because they can stand up!*

At that time in my life I was just beginning to grow as a Christian, and my hunger for spiritual food spurred me to spend a good deal of time in the Bible. A bite of that food went down pretty hard one day—some spiritual spinach which tasted bad at first, but which I learned to appreciate later as I grew up in the Lord. My meal was served from John's Gospel, chapter twenty-one, where it seems Peter had the same problem I did. One of his friends appeared to be getting a better deal in life than he was! Jesus had just announced to Peter that years in the future he would be led to a martyr's death, but not a word had been spoken about John.

Perhaps jealousy stirred in Peter's heart. Wasn't John the one who'd gotten to sit next to Jesus at the Last Supper, the one who seemed to be especially intimate with the Master? Was Christ going to let John off with an easy death in his old age and an exciting ministry while he lived? It was too much for Peter to keep inside. "What about him?" Peter asked Jesus, pointing to John. "What's his future going to be like?"

The answer Jesus gave shocked me. I certainly would have expected a response like: "Don't worry,

Peter. I'll be with you through whatever. Everything's going to be all right." But what He actually replied was more in this vein: "Look, if it's My will that John lives until I come again, what is that to you? What I have planned for John is not your business—your business is to make sure your own heart and life are right. So stop grumbling and follow Me!"

Now this sounds harsh at first. But when I thought about it, I began to see that Jesus was right in being so stern. In the first place, self-pity never helps anyone. It only magnifies a person's own misery. And it certainly doesn't help God. Can you imagine how ineffective Peter would have been as a preacher if every time he was scheduled to speak he was backstage sobbing for himself, wondering if this would be the sermon that would anger people to the point of killing him? In the second place, by comparing his situation with John's and demanding that God give them "equal rights," Peter was doubting that God's plan for him was good. And that is sin, for "without faith it is impossible to please God, because anyone who comes to him must believe that . . . he rewards those who earnestly seek him" (Heb. 11:6). To doubt God's good intentions is to sing: "Jesus hates me this I know, for my unbelief tells me so."

Besides, although it may seem God is being grossly unfair and is giving us a heavier cross to bear, we really don't know what the person next door has to live with. I may be grieved with a broken neck envying my healthy neighbor, never knowing that my neighbor is grieving with a broken heart. Peter probably had no idea that John, in his old age, would spend years languishing in an island prison, receiving the visions of the Book of Revelation. There John would gaze with longing upon the waiting glories of heaven, upon the special honors given to the martyrs (including Peter himself!) around God's throne, and would wish that his life, too, had been mercifully cut short.[7]

Because we don't have all the facts about how much each person has suffered, or what sins they need chastening for, or what qualities they do or don't need built into their lives, we just can't say what trials each person should be getting—or how many! But though *we* don't have all the facts, God does, and "Shall not the Judge of all the earth deal justly?" (Gen. 18:25). God is doing in each one of our lives something expressly different than He is doing in another's. He will give us the unique grace to bear our unique cross.

I'm excited to say that today Sheryl is still a part of an intimate circle of friends with whom I have real and deep fellowship—only minus the envy, thanks to Christ's words to Peter. When you think about it, wouldn't it be awful if, whenever we had deep trials, God allowed all our friends to be going through exactly the same problems? Who would be there to lift us up? Doesn't it make far more sense, instead of envying our friends who have lighter loads, to benefit from their supportive fellowship?

Fellowship

We should never be alone when we suffer. I don't mean never for a minute, or that we must not live in an apartment by ourselves. But we should never build a self-imposed wall around us that allows absolutely no one inside to see what we're going through and to hurt with our hurts. God never intended that we shoulder the load of suffering by ourselves. "Two are better than one. . . . For if either of them falls, one will lift up his companion. But woe to the one who falls where there is not another to lift him up" (Eccl. 4:9-10).

If you are single or widowed, you may feel as though such an intimate sharing of sorrows is impossible. But you do have a family—other Christians, the body of Christ. This family of believers is meant to be one of the warmest and most intimate circles of friendship in the world. I believe, and am told by my married friends, that even for a married person it is a mistake to try and rely on one's partner as one's total source of fellowship. God deliberately designed the church to consist of young and old, male and female, all types of people, and we need to rub shoulders with them all if our innermost needs are to be met. I absolutely could not make it without the sharing and caring of the Christian friends I have made in my church and community—friends of all ages.

Perhaps the saddest thing is to see Christian leaders who feel they cannot share any of their trials with those in the church who are under their spiritual care. Granted, none of us can reveal *all* our most private concerns to *everyone*. But we do need to share them with *someone*. And perhaps some should be shared with the congregation at large, or certainly more than are usually shared. The idea that Christian leaders should be towers of strength who never admit to their own pains and sorrows doesn't come from the Bible. Paul boasted freely of his pains and weaknesses and frequently asked for prayer. A Christian leader who never shares his problems with those under his care teaches them by example to do the same thing!

But what if your relationships with friends and church members aren't as open as you'd like them to be? Then it's up to you to do something about it. *Fellowship is usually created, not found!* My friend Diana taught me so much about this when I was in high school. Diana was the type of person who felt like clawing the walls if a conversation never moved beyond the trivial. Not that she couldn't let her hair down and have fun. Far from it! But she had a way of getting people to share honestly their thoughts and feelings. I think her secret was that she really listened to people when they talked and asked them questions about *them*. Her facial expression showed that she really was interested—no wandering eyes or anything.

But Diana did more than listen. She shared. Now sharing your deep thoughts, fears, and concerns with another person is a scary thing. It's making yourself vulnerable. But isn't that much of what love is all about? Vulnerability. Diana tactfully and lovingly "invaded" the world of the people she met and knew and taught us something about what real fellowship is all about. She would say things like, "Why don't we pray together for just a minute before you leave?" People who are suffering are in desperate need of deep and meaningful conversations with other believers. They shouldn't have to endure a constant diet of trite dialogue when they are around other Christians. They get enough of that out in the world.

When you suffer, there's something else you can do to foster close sharing and contact with other Christians. You can pray for it.

Not long ago the choir of a Christian college was touring some eastern states during spring vacation and gave a concert one evening at a church in our area. After the concert, the singers were assigned in groups of two or three to various families in the church who would house them for the night. Two girls were assigned to Mr. and Mrs. Estes, parents of my friend Steve.

As the four of them sat around the living room chatting and enjoying refreshments, Mr. Estes and his wife began bringing Christ into the conversation in their warm and tactful manner, asking the girls how they had met the Lord and what He was doing in their lives. To their hosts' surprise the two students looked at each other, smiled, and then let out a squeal of delight.

"Mr. and Mrs. Estes," the younger one exclaimed, "you don't know how glad I am you asked these questions." With that, she began sharing with them something of her background. She had become a Christian less than a year before. After that, naturally her thoughts and concern turned toward her parents. She wanted them to have the same personal relationship with Christ that she had, but they didn't seem interested. For weeks she unsuccessfully tried to persuade her dad to go to church with her until one Sunday morning he finally agreed.

The service that day seemed to touch his heart. The people were friendly, the sermon appropriate—everything was perfect. In the vestibule afterward her father said, "I must say that the service today really moved me. Maybe I'll come around to seeing things your way in time. Just don't rush me." Inside the girl beamed with joy, said a prayer of thanks to God, and promised herself she would never force things on her father.

The family was just getting into the car when a gentleman approached them from the other side of the parking lot and hollered a greeting to her dad. The man turned out to be one of the church elders, someone her father had casually met a few times at his place of business.

"Say, how are you doing?" the elder asked as he smiled and extended a hand to her father. "Good to have you here. I see you've brought your wife and family," he said, bending down and nodding to them through the car window. Then he said something to her father which made the girl cringe.

"Hey, why not give me a call sometime and we'll get together and have a few drinks, okay? Well, gotta go. Take care," he waved, and off he went.

As her father got into the car and shut the door, the look on his face made the atmosphere so tense you could almost see it.

"You know," he said to his daughter as they pulled out of the lot, "I thought this place and these people were for real. But they're no different from me." With that he shut his heart to the gospel and never returned to church or discussed spiritual things with her again. In fact, her family had become so hostile to her new-found faith in Christ that when she and a friend arrived at her family's summer home that Easter for vacation, they politely requested that she leave.

"And that's why I'm here on this tour, Mr. and Mrs. Estes, instead of at home with my family this Easter," she concluded. "I've been really aching to talk to someone about all these things. The people whose homes I have stayed at this week have been very nice, but all we ever talked about was the weather. So my friend and I prayed this afternoon that we'd get assigned to a home tonight where I could really unburden my heart and where we could share and pray together! So when you moved the conversation in the direction you did, well . . . I just sort of exploded with joy!"

You see what happens when we ask God to send us fellowship and when someone reaches out to make that fellowship happen? Sharing with other Christians—it's one of the best responses to suffering I know!

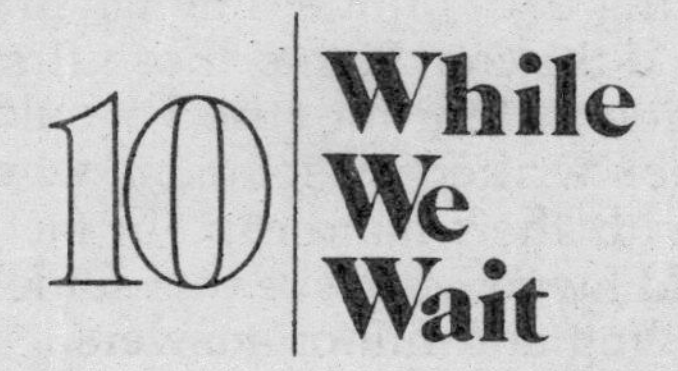

10 While We Wait

It's All Right to Cry

When my first book, *Joni,* came out in 1976, I had no idea God would use it in as many lives as He did. As a result I've been deluged with interesting mail, ranging from simple order forms for my artwork to friendly personal letters to distressed pleas for help. Some of those pleas sound like this:

> Dear Joni,
>
> I have a nephew who recently broke his neck and is now paralyzed. He's so depressed and keeps asking "Why?!" I thought maybe you might autograph him a copy of your book. Do you think you could also write him a little note with a few tips on how to cope?
>
> Thank you.

My heart goes out to such people. It is frustrating to stand beside the bed of a suffering loved one and not be able to do anything. How good it would feel to be able to give a helpful book, or to share just the right encouraging word. But although I sympathize with those who are in this situation, I'm not sure that a book or a letter from me, or anyone, is the right prescription.

In the first place, a person usually isn't ready for

advice and insights just after something drastic has happened to him. Thinking back on the time when I was seventeen, lying in a Stryker Frame those first few weeks after the accident, I'm not sure I would have been ready for a book written by someone who had successfully dealt with their handicap. In fact, the *last* thing in the world I wanted to see was someone in a wheelchair, smiling and full of answers.

At first it may seem that a person who has just lost a leg, discovered he has terminal cancer, or broken his neck is desperately looking for answers. "Why did this happen to me?!" he cries, and so we jump right in and give him sixteen biblical reasons why it happened. But more often than not, when he first asks "Why?" he doesn't really mean it as a question. He means it as an emotional release—sometimes even as an accusation. It's not the genuine "Why?" of a searching heart, but the bitter "Why?!" of a clenched fist.

It takes *time* for a person to realize that he never will walk again, or that he really does have terminal cancer, or whatever. After he has had time to cry, to agonize, and to sort out his feelings, *then* he gets into an "asking mood," and then our advice and counsel is helpful.

I think one of the reasons Steve was able to help me so much in dealing with my paralysis was that we met two full years after my accident—long enough for me to begin asking questions and begin listening to the answers. Others tried to give me the same help earlier, but I just wasn't ready for it.

There's another reason I wouldn't send books and Bible verses the instant a person has some terrible accident or illness. I wouldn't want him to think I was saying, "No, no! Stop your crying. Dry those tears and listen to all these Bible passages about suffering. Then you won't feel bad any more." I wouldn't want to give the impression that we are to learn what the Bible has to say about the value of suffering *instead of* feeling grief and sorrow. I have read books and heard speakers that implied that if we were really giving thanks for all things and seeing our sufferings in the light of God's Word, they wouldn't even seem like sufferings. But that sort of unrealistic, happy-go-lucky approach to trials can't be found in the Bible. "Giving thanks in all things" is not the same as "feeling like a million dollars in all things." We have the freedom to feel sorrow and grief.

Let me illustrate. This past year a friend of mine, Jeanette, and her husband lost their three-year-old son to cancer. Cute little Bradley, blond and blue-eyed—for a year and a half his parents had known death was coming. And, of course, when he died their grief was very deep. But throughout the whole ordeal they were never bitter toward God. They continued to love and serve Him, trusting completely that He cared for them and knew what He was doing.

About two weeks after Bradley's funeral Jeanette attended a women's Bible study at her church. Afterwards, as she walked down the hall with some other ladies, she spotted a little boy standing tiptoe atop some small steps, straining to sip from the water fountain. The sight immediately recalled memories of her own little Bradley who had always made a big production of climbing the little stairs to drink from that very fountain. She began to sob.

Walking beside her was one of her closest friends who sensed what had happened. This friend didn't say a word, just put her arms around Jeanette and silently held and comforted her. It was what she needed.

Then another woman, who didn't know Jeanette, saw her crying and obviously wanted to help. Coming up, she patted Jeanette and said, "I'm praying for you, honey. Praise the Lord."

The words stung like fire.

Later, Jeanette expressed how she felt at that moment. "I really had to ask God to help me with my feelings about that woman. I know she only wanted to help. But the way she said 'Praise the Lord' made me feel like I didn't have any right to cry if I was trusting the Lord." Pausing for a moment, she thoughtfully added, "Maybe she just didn't know that trusting the Lord doesn't rule out crying. Maybe she forgot that God told us to weep with those who weep."[8]

Jeanette was right. After all, Jesus wept at the reality of death when He stood at the grave of His friend Lazarus. Even though we will one day be raised to life, death is a horrible thing. All the sufferings of this earth are horrible things. It's foolish to think Christians can benefit from their trials without *feeling* them. And when Jesus shed those tears at His friend's tomb, He showed us that it's all right to grieve.

God doesn't ask us to stifle our tears. Let's not ask it from each other. For there is "a time to weep . . . a time to mourn" (Eccl. 3:4).

Songs in the Night

But mourning isn't enough. When your body is racked with pain, your heart is breaking with sorrow, your mind is a mass of confusion, and your soul is weighted with guilt, you have a need to know there is someone, anyone, who understands what you're going through. Well, one of the best places you can find this understanding is the Book of Psalms. This is no ordinary book, for many of the psalms were written out of the depths of despair, and they are meant to be read during the depths of despair.

David, the poet behind many of the psalms, knew what it was to suffer. In his early years, his life hung on a thread as the armies of Saul pursued him like a common criminal. He lost his best friend, Jonathan, in battle. After becoming king he was gnawed by the guilt of having committed adultery and murder. One of his sons died in infancy. For the rest of his life, his family and kingdom were plagued with incest, rebellion, murder, and war. Here's a man who really had problems!

Most of David's psalms don't supply any answers to our problems. Many of them are merely detailed and desperate pleas to God for help. But when I sit down and read the prayers of this man (and of the other psalmists, too), I know I am not alone. Here is someone who understands the way I feel—someone who felt the way I feel.

It's as if David and I are sitting together on a rock in the field beside his sheep. I listen as he, with all his poetic skill, pours out to God the aching of his heart. In doing so, he pours out my aching as well. *Yes,* I think, *those words capture what I am thinking. That's what I want to pray.* And it lets me know God has heard and understood my thoughts.

Listen as David groans before God in Psalm 6:

> I am weary with my sighing;
> Every night I make my bed swim,
> I dissolve my couch with my tears.
> (Ps. 6:6)

Doesn't that perfectly describe some sorrowful nights when your own pillow has been drenched with tears? Can't you feel with him as he cries out to God in anxiety and guilt in Psalm 38?

> For I am ready to fall,
> And my sorrow is continually before me.
> For I confess my iniquity;

I am full of anxiety because of my sin. . . .
Do not forsake me, O Lord;
O my God, do not be far from me!
(Ps. 38:17-18, 21)

As we spend more and more time with David, we trust our feelings to him because we see a man who has gone through what we're going through. So when his hopelessness turns into assurance that God has heard his prayers, his confidence becomes ours. Then we can say with him:

Lord, all my desire is before Thee;
And my sighing is not hidden from Thee.
(Ps. 38:9)

The pain is still there. Yet the flicker of light refuses to die regardless of how much rain and sorrow is poured on it:

For I hope in Thee, O Lord;
Thou wilt answer, O Lord my God.
(Ps. 38:15)

If David could hope like that, can't I? If the man who was an adulterer and murderer was able to face God with confidence despite his sins, can't I? That's worth shouting about! And sometimes David does just that. Like a refreshing summer shower in the middle of a heat wave, his sorrow turns to joy and he utters:

I waited patiently for the Lord;
And He inclined to me, and heard my cry.
He brought me up out of the pit of destruction,
out of the miry clay;
And He set my feet upon a rock making my footsteps
firm.
And He put a new song in my mouth,
a song of praise to our God.
(Ps. 40:1-3)

Seeing the change in David's life makes us feel that we, too, can have strength to wait patiently for the Lord, that He will hear *our* cry, set *our* feet upon a rock, and give *us* a song. When we have heard this once-discouraged shepherd say:

> Thou hast turned for me my mourning into dancing;
> Thou hast loosed my sackcloth and girded me with gladness.
> (Ps. 30:11)

we are able to believe that we, too, will one day laugh again. When he writes:

> Weeping may last for the night,
> But a shout of joy comes in the morning,
> (Ps. 30:5)

we begin to believe what before we could never believe—that our own crises, too, will eventually pass. And when we have heard this poet who so graphically expressed the dreadfulness of a sleepless night write:

> I lay down and slept;
> I awoke, for the Lord sustains me,
> (Ps. 3:5)

we, too, feel able to fall asleep at last. Somehow, God uses those soothing psalms to turn our tears of agony into tears of release. Like a person who feels better after he has cried and "gotten it all out," so the Psalms help us get things out—expressing to God our deep anguish and assuring our troubled souls that He is still worth trusting.

Waiting on God

Six years ago my family and I boarded a chair-lift that cabled us to the top of a huge, glacier-scarred mountain overlooking the wilderness reserve of Jasper Provincial Park in Alberta, Canada. There our eyes met the spectacle of majestic pine forests, wild rugged terrain, and turquoise lakes. Shivering beneath our down jackets, half from the icy cold and half from the awesome view, we yelled our delight to one another over the violent roaring of the wind.

I marveled at the sight of a soaring eagle moving far across the wooded valley, a tiny speck against the distant mountain range. I watched as he circled and dove, admiring his grace and ease.

Eagles seem to have to do with big things—mountains, canyons, great depths, immense heights. It's always at the most stupendous and alluring spectacles of nature that we find them.

God talks about eagles. In one of the most well-loved passages of the Old Testament, He uses their flight to describe the adventure that will unfold to the suffering Christian who waits for Him.

> Though youths grow weary and tired,
> And vigorous young men stumble badly,
> Yet those who wait for the Lord
> Will gain new strength;
> They will mount up with wings like eagles,
> They will run and not get tired,
> They will walk and not become weary.
> (Isa. 40:30-31)

What does it mean to "wait for the Lord"? Well, some people think of the kind of waiting you do because you're forced to. (Like when there are ten people ahead of you in the waiting room at the doctor's office, and so you kill time flipping through magazines.) But when the Bible talks about waiting, it means *confidently trusting* that God knows how much suffering I need and can take. It means *looking expectantly* toward the time when He will free me from my burdens.

But not get weary? Not tire or stumble? How can that be when these are the very trademarks of those who suffer? Yet God's promise is clear that those who wait for Him in their sufferings will receive strength and endurance which others know nothing of.

Due to my condition, you'd think I would grow weary, weak, and tired of life. But because I know God and confidently look forward to the day when He will give me a new body, I am able to "mount up with wings like an eagle" even now. My expectancy gives me endurance and strength, like that of an eagle who with powerful wings is able to venture out in the mighty wind currents that whip through the canyons.

Oh, yes. There's one more way that waiting on God makes me like an eagle. My body is held by the limits of this chair. But the waiting hope I have in God's future for me gives me the freedom to soar to heights of joy and explore the canyon depths of God's tender mercies.

* * * *

A year after I was released from the hospital I read the inspiring story of a French noblewoman named Madame Guyon. This saintly woman was arrested in 1688 and falsely accused of heresy, sorcery, and adultery by jealous church officials. She was convicted, and as a result spent the next ten years in prison. During those long and lonely years of her confinement, she penned the following poem. It is an eloquent expression of the strength God will give to the suffering heart that waits on Him.

> A little bird I am,
> Shut from the fields of air;
> And in my cage I sit and sing
> To Him who placed me there;
> Well pleased a prisoner to be
> Because, my God, it pleases Thee.

Naught have I else to do;
I sing the whole day long;
And He whom most I love to please,
Doth listen to my song:
He caught and bound my wandering wing,
But still He bends to hear me sing.

My cage confines me round;
Abroad I cannot fly;
But though my wing is closely bound,
My heart's at liberty;
My prison walls cannot control
The flight, the freedom of the soul.

Oh! it is good to soar
These bolts and bars above,
To Him whose purpose I adore,
Whose providence I love;
And in Thy mighty will to find
The joy, the freedom, of the mind.

HEALING: A PIECE OF THE PUZZLE?

11 I Wish I Were Healed

It's a rather quiet afternoon around our house today. The yellow school bus full of chattering students won't drop off my niece, Kay, for at least another hour. Through the bay window of my drawing studio I can see my green-thumbed sister, Jay, out in the garden mothering her radishes and zucchini squash. No friends or visitors have dropped by today—a rare thing at our house—so I have the place all to myself. It's a perfect time to catch up on some reading.

On the far corner of the desk at which I am seated lies a book I've been wanting to get into recently. It looks just within nudging reach. I use the word "nudging" because I don't have the use of my hands or fingers. What I can do is position my arm beside the book and with weak, awkward, jerky motions manipulate it toward me. It took me a long time after my accident to learn to do this, so I'm grateful for the ability to nudge. I can even turn the pages and keep them open by myself if the binding of the book is broken in.

But today, as my brace-supported arm inches past the pencil holder toward the book, I can see a potential problem—the small paperback is just on the borderline of being out of reach. *Uh-oh. This is going to take some stretching.* I can get my wrist beside it but not quite behind it to pull it my way. I need some strategy. *Hey, maybe I can zigzag it.* My cousin Eddie once taught me about sailing. "When you want to head a sailboat into the wind," he said, "you can't just head straight on. You need to weave your boat right, then left, back and forth, and inch your way forward." He called it tacking.

I'm going to tack. I'll push the book left to the edge of the desk. Then I'll push it right. I'll move it slightly back each time until it gets close enough to open. Handicapped people have to get used to little tasks becoming big chores.

But I'm not sure I'll ever get used to failing at tasks that even a handicapped person can usually accomplish. Today that little book is just an inch and a half farther away than I'm used to reaching. I can move it, but not towards me. *Come on, book, cooperate.* Every nudge seems to push it farther away. My only hope is to try to press the weight of my arm downward on top of the cover and attempt a quick jerk back towards me. With studied effort I place my wrist on the book, strain with weak muscles to push down as hard as I can, and pull back fast!

But all I succeed in doing is knocking the book off the table. *Oh, no! Book, there you are within eight inches of my dangling left arm, and I can't touch you.* I glance out the window. Jay's still outside. *She'd never hear me yell from in here.* Nobody's there to pick it up. No other book is within reach. So I will spend the next sixty minutes sitting exasperated at the desk, staring at the bookshelf, spending an anticipated hour of reading with nothing to do.

It's at times like this I wish I were healed. Please realize that I don't always feel this way—not even

At work on one of her latest drawings

Wisdom is a tree of life
to them that lay hold
upon her.
Proverbs 3:18

Charlotte Sherman (left) and Betsy work on mail at the JONI PTL office

Frank and Diana Mood discuss the new book with Steve and Joni

Jay

Joni and friend Dick Filbert

Photo by Olin A Kinney

Addressing World Vision Conference, 1977

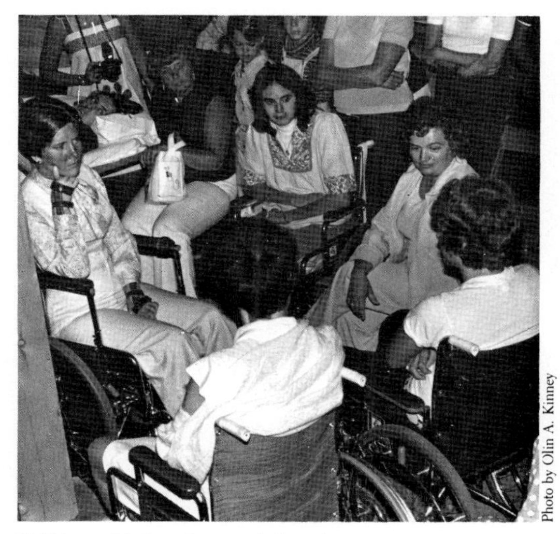

Photo by Olin A. Kinney

Talking with handicapped friends

Photo by Russ Busby

Billy Graham and Joni at Billy Graham Crusade, 1977

Photo by Russ Busby

Joni, Kathy, and Jay

He that believes on me
out of him shall flow
rivers of living water.
John 7:38

often. But on days like today it sure would help! I call them "I-wish-I-had-my-hands-back" days. Though I have learned to be content with my condition, and even to rejoice in it, the prospect of being restored to a normal life would be very exciting. I think in all honesty that any handicapped person, Christian or otherwise, would rather be well. So naturally, once my relationship with God began to get straightened out, and once I learned that regaining the use of my hands and legs was beyond medical hope, I became vitally interested in what the Bible might have to say about miraculous healing.

I began investigating in every way I could—studying the Scriptures, reading books, and gleaning counsel and advice from friends and various Christian leaders. What everyone agreed upon was the fact that God certainly *can* heal any person, no matter how serious the problem.

But what they could not agree on was whether or not God *wills* to heal all those who truly come to Him in faith. I found two extreme opposite positions. On one end of the spectrum were those who stated that the age of miracles is absolutely past and gone and that we should never seek and expect them today. At the other end were those who felt that miracles can be a part of the everyday life of each Christian and that healing from disease is an important portion of the believer's heritage. Between those two opposite poles, I found Christians at all points. This controversy continues in Christian circles right up to today. And I want to emphasize that there are believers on both sides of the fence who are totally dedicated to Jesus Christ as Lord and to the Bible as God's Word. This is not a discussion between people who love God and people who don't, between "the good guys" and "the bad guys." It is a kind of intramural debate.

With all these opinions facing me, I began narrowing down the possibilities. To start with, I just couldn't go along with those who were positive that God never heals anyone miraculously today. In the first place, who is in a position to say this? Just because I may not know of anyone whom God has healed in an extraordinary way, does that prove He has never done so during my lifetime? God deals with His children as He wills. To one He gives a life of relative ease and comfort; to another He gives the privilege of suffering for Him in a concentration camp. For some, He rewards their faith in this life; for others, He waits until after they die (Heb. 11:32-39). I cannot take my own experience from the hand of God and set it up as the absolute norm for His dealing with others. For me to say with certainty that God has not supernaturally healed anyone during my lifetime would mean that I'd have to be at every single place to check out every alleged healing.

Besides, what about all the testimonies from Christians who claim they have been divinely healed? One such person is a personal friend of mine, a mature Christian lady who suffered from a severe bone marrow disease. Every known medical procedure having failed, the doctors gave her a short time to live. But she and others prayed, and when she returned to the doctor for examination he dropped his jaw in amazement. This man was not a believer in Christ, but after taking repeated blood tests over a period of time he told my friend, "There is no natural or medical explanation I can give. Your situation was beyond hope. All I can say is that this is a miracle." That was fifteen years ago, and she is still healthy today. I know this woman well enough to feel confident she is not lying to me nor was she deceived into believing something that never really happened.

Of course, it's possible that some of these testimonies of healing come from people who just *think* they have been healed—over-emotional people, perhaps. Some may have even lied in order to receive attention. And several biblical passages (e.g., Matt. 7:22-23; Matt. 24:24; 2 Thess. 2:9) imply that some of these miracles may even come from Satan. But to place everybody into such categories is something I am not prepared to do.

Earlier I said there is only one way a person could be sure that no miracles of healing ever occurred during his lifetime—he would have to have been present with all persons at all times. Actually there is another way. Suppose there was a promise in God's Word that He would not miraculously heal anyone after a given point in time. Then we could be absolutely certain that any so-called divine healing after that was either a hoax or from Satan. There are a number of Christians who feel this is, in fact, what the Scriptures teach. And as a result, they write off each and every healing testimony no matter how convincing.

I've got to say here that I really agree with people who insist on judging experiences by the light of Scripture and not vice versa. Modern Christians tend to put too much weight on their experiences anyway. Then they set their conclusions up as some kind of absolute truth by which everything else is to be interpreted, putting those experiences on an equal level with Scripture.

But this *doesn't* mean we should totally *ignore* our experiences. There are far too many who have claimed to have experienced miraculous healing for us to just write them off. Lots of these testimonies come from people who are mature in the faith—and many are from the field of medicine. All this should flash a yellow light in our minds if we're among those who feel the Bible totally rules out miracles for our day. It should make us go back and be sure we have understood God's Word correctly.

So at least for the present, I myself have had to rule out that pole of the spectrum which says God never heals miraculously today. In my opinion the Bible doesn't teach it, and experience doesn't support it.

* * * *

But what about the other position—the view which says not only is healing for today, but it is for everyone? What about the claim that none will be turned away who truly have faith in Jesus to heal their body?

Not long after I broke my neck, some of my friends and others who knew of my condition began sharing with me that they felt just this way. To this day I receive scores of letters from Christians who share the same conviction. Some have sent books. Many have taken the time to compile Scripture references in support of the idea that I not only could, but should be healed. Here are a few quotes:

> ". . . To get right to the point, I believe you could be healed, Joni. I'm not sure what you've been taught, or where you stand on the subject, but there are many scriptures saying that healing is for today and that it is for everyone, whatever their condition. . . ."

> "I have heard that you believe God wants you in the shape you're in, but I can't believe that. Here's why . . . [at this point, numerous scriptural supports are given]. Joni, you might say you are glorifying God in your paralysis, but how much more in your healing! When Jesus healed people, the Bible says they glorified God after they were healed. You are known all over the world, and if you were healed, can you imagine how fantastic a thing it would be? Can you imagine how much more God would be glorified?

> ". . . John 10:10 says we are to have an abundant life. Being paralyzed, can you honestly say you are having an abundant life? Jesus came to set people free. You're bound to your wheelchair. Your body is the temple of the Holy Spirit. Do you think He wants His temple to be broken and helpless? . . ."
>
> ". . . I'd like to see one more chapter written in your book. I'd like the heading to be, 'How God Healed Me.'"

It would be impractical to list here all of the reasons I have been given why any Christian can expect healing from God if he truly believes. But from the number of letters I've received, books I've read, and discussions I've had, here is a summary of the more common points posed to me:

1) Sickness and death are the work of Satan and his forces (Luke 13:16; Acts 10:38). Since the whole purpose of Jesus' coming was to destroy the works of the devil (1 John 3:8), those who believe in Jesus can expect freedom from disease.

2) Jesus healed people during His lifetime. Verses like Hebrews 13:8 tell us that God never changes, that Jesus Christ is "the same yesterday, today, and forever." Therefore, He must still be in the business of healing people today as He did centuries ago.

3) We have promises in Scripture that whatever we ask in Jesus' name will be done for us (John 14:12-14; Mark 11:22-24; 1 John 3:22 and many others). These promises would seem to include prayers for healing.

4) There are a number of Scripture passages which specifically guarantee the health and healing of believers. The most well-known is Isaiah 53:5, "By His scourging we are healed." Others are Psalm 103:1-3 ("Bless the Lord, O my soul. . . . Who heals all your diseases"), 1 Peter 2:24, and James 5:15.

These points which others had shared seemed to make sense. *Guess that answers my question about where I should go from here,* I thought to myself. Having considered the issue, I became convinced healing was for me.

12 Why Wasn't I Healed?

On a rainy afternoon in the early summer of 1972 about fifteen people gathered together in a tiny oak church not far from my home. The group consisted of close friends, family, and church leaders—several elders and a few ordained ministers—whom I had called together to pray for my healing. It was a simple format. We began by reading aloud in turn from various Scriptures. Some read from the New Testament . . .

> "We have this assurance in approaching God, that if we ask anything according to his will, he hears us. And if we know that he hears us—whatever we ask—we know that we have what we ask of him" (1 John 5:14-15).

some from the Old Testament . . .

> "But those who look to the Lord will renew their strength. They will soar on wings like eagles; they will run and not grow weary, they will walk and not faint" (Isa. 40:31, NIV).

several read promises about healing . . .

> "Is any one of you sick? He should call the elders of the church to pray over him and anoint him

> with oil in the name of the Lord. And the prayer offered in faith will make the sick person well; the Lord will raise him up . . ." (James 5:14-15).

others read the stories of those who were healed . . .

> ". . . He said to the paralytic, 'I tell you, get up, take your mat and go home.' He got up, took his mat and walked out in full view of them all. This amazed everyone and they praised God, saying, 'We have never seen anything like this!'" (Mark 2:1-12).

After the readings, they anointed my head with olive oil. Then followed a time of direct, fervent, believing prayer for my healing. We asked God to glorify Himself by allowing me to walk again, and we trusted Him to do so.

By the time our brief service was over, the rain had stopped. Exiting through the front doors of the church, we were greeted by a beautiful rainbow in the misty distance, sparkling from a bath in golden sunlight. I cannot say it was an extremely emotional moment for any of us, but it gave me just one more reassurance that God was looking down on us right there and had heard our prayers.

I left the church parking lot in exactly the same frame of mind that I had entered it—fully expecting God to heal me. "Thank You, Lord," I prayed silently as the car pulled out, praising God for what I was convinced He had already begun to do.

* * * *

A week went by . . . then another . . . then another. My body still hadn't gotten the message that I was healed. Fingers and toes still didn't respond to the mental command, "Move!" *Perhaps it's going to be a gradual thing,* I reasoned, *a slow process of steady recovery.* I continued to wait. But three weeks became a month, and one month became two.

You can imagine the questions that began popping into my mind. *Is there some sin in my life?* Well, of course, there is still sin in every Christian's life. No one is without it. But there was no area of conscious rebellion against God on my part. I was living in close fellowship with Him, keeping short accounts, confessing my sins and failures to Him daily and receiving assurances of forgiveness.

Had we done things right? My friend Betsy assured me on that point when I asked her.

"Of course we did, Joni," she defended. "That wasn't some off-beat group of immature Christians trying to do something apart from the authority of church leaders. Ordained men and elders led the meeting."

"I guess you're right," I nodded in agreement. "We did things just like it says to do in James 5 and other places."

But then came to my mind the ten-thousand-dollar question, the question that is in the minds of so many I've met over the years who have not been healed in response to their prayers—*Did I have enough faith?*

What a flood of guilt that question brings. It constantly leaves the door open for the despairing thought: *God didn't heal me because there is something wrong with me. I must not have believed hard enough.* You can easily see how this can produce a vicious cycle:

A Christian who is afflicted with some sort of physical problem asks a friend, "Do you think God would heal me if I asked Him?"

"Of course He will," the friend assures him. "But you mustn't doubt. The slightest trace of doubt may prevent your being healed."

So knowing that "faith comes by hearing, and hearing by the Word of God," the ill person spends hours in the Bible, reading about God's mighty power and wonderful promises, in order to strengthen his faith. Finally, he feels ready to pray. He prays by himself, with the elders of his church, at a healing service, or whatever, but he doesn't get healed.

"What happened? What went wrong?" he asks. Often he is told, "The problem isn't with God. He's always ready and waiting. The blame must be yours. You probably didn't really let your faith go and trust God all the way." Yet the poor guy *knows* he believed God in that prayer for healing more than he's ever believed God in his life.

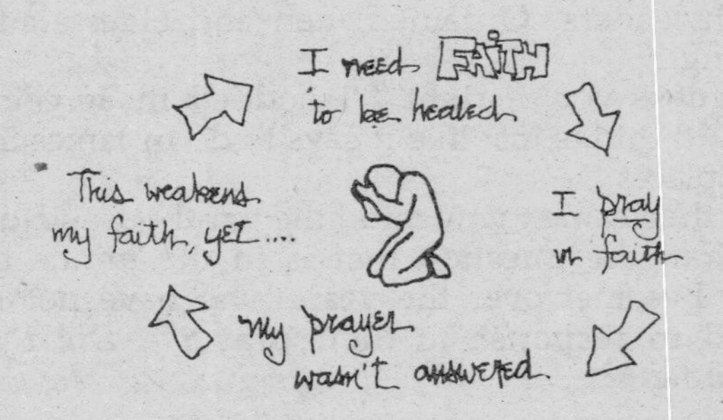

What is the result going to be? Since he didn't get healed, naturally he begins to wonder if God really intends it. His faith has weakened. Yet he's been told that more faith is just what He needs to get healed. Each unanswered prayer makes him doubt more and more, which in turn makes his chances for healing less and less! It becomes a losing battle.

But thinking about it, I knew I had entered the prayer service in that little church with total faith that God would heal me. I had even surprised various friends by calling the week before and warning, "Watch for me standing on your doorstep soon; I'm going to be healed."

No, insufficient faith was not the missing ingredient. The answer must lie elsewhere.

Since that time I have had years in a wheelchair to ponder the question, "Why wasn't I healed?—time to read many books, talk with many people, and do much prayerful considering and studying of Scripture. I still don't have all the answers about healing. But I do have some of them—answers that come from the Bible and that have been of great personal help to me. In a moment I'll share with you the conclusions I've reached after my six-year search for answers, and what led to those conclusions.

But first, let me give a warning. Often we have questions about issues like this which require more than just simple answers, but we don't have the patience to hear those answers out. Sometimes in the past, my own attitude has been, "Don't give me any detailed theological stuff. Just answer my question." Then, because I refused to take the time or mental energy to hear and consider the answer, I would go away assuming no answer existed.

It's so easy to take a casual, surface approach to the Bible when searching for answers. We meander through its pages with a lazy mental attitude, taking things out of context and failing to understand figures of speech. But Paul tells us to correctly handle the word of truth (2 Tim. 2:15). Apparently, it's possible to *incorrectly* handle it. In 2 Peter 3:15-16, the apostle Peter warns us not to distort the Scriptures, reminding us that some things in the Bible are just plain hard to understand. We need to treat God's Word with respect, digging hard to find the intended meaning. This is especially true when studying something as controversial and charged with emotion as the miraculous healing issue.

With this in mind, here is the conclusion I've come to regarding miraculous healing: God certainly can, and sometimes does, heal people in a miraculous way today. But the Bible does *not* teach that He will *always* heal those who come to Him in faith. He sovereignly reserves the right to heal or not to heal as He sees fit.

To understand how I reached that conclusion, ask yourself this question: "Just what is disease?"* I don't mean "What is it medically?" nor "What is its physical cause?" I mean "What is it biblically? Why is it here? What is its purpose?" The answers to these questions will shed a lot of light on the subject of healing. And to find the answers, we need to go all the way back to our first parents and the Garden of Eden.

In the beginning God created the universe and gave the earth to man, appointing him as His "assistant ruler" over earth (Gen. 1:26). Adam and Eve ruled the earth under God's authority. There was no sin and, therefore, none of sin's awful results. Pollution was nonexistent. Nature was helpful, not hostile, to man. No hurricanes, floods, tidal waves, or

---

*I am using the word "disease" throughout these next few chapters to include all physical problems and disorders: sickness, deformities, handicaps, loss of limbs, pain, etc.

volcanic eruptions threatened man's survival. Death and disease were unknown. There was no fear that one of Eden's luscious-looking fruits might secretly contain some fatal poison. For both humans and the world of nature it was truly Paradise.

But earth did not remain a paradise for long. Satan, who had rebelled against God in a prideful struggle, followed by his army of demons, had set up a rival kingdom against God. Planet earth became his headquarters. Mankind was enticed to sin, to eat the forbidden fruit, and as a result a curse fell upon the earth. Romans 8:20-23 makes it clear that not only man but the earth itself—the world of nature—became subject to futility and frustration, to the endless cycle of change and decay. It seems quite possible that before this time all animals may have been vegetarians. Now they fed upon one another, and violence brought about the law of the jungle.

Nature not only became hostile to itself but to man as well. Once they had worked together; now they were in conflict. Once the earth had yielded its fruit without much effort from man; now it became a world of weeds! Wild animals sought man's life, and floods and droughts threatened to wipe him out.

Man himself began to experience problems in both soul and body as a result of sin. Immediately after disobeying God, Adam and Eve began feeling guilty because they *were* guilty. This caused the world's first marital argument— Adam blamed Eve for his sin. Loneliness, frustration, sorrow, and all the internal problems people face began right there. Jealousy and murder were not long in coming. All humans forever after were born with a sinful nature, separated from God and spiritually dead.

Just as thorns and thistles attacked the earth, sickness and weakness attacked man's body. As we read through the Book of Genesis, the human life span becomes shorter and shorter. No longer did people live hundreds of years as the early generations did. Illness and disease infested the world. Deformed babies and retarded children became a fact of life. And worst of all—the whole process ended in death. Plants died. Animals died. People died.

Yes, sin brought its own special consequences and results. Satan became the king of planet earth, the "god of this age" (2 Cor. 4:4), the "ruler of the kingdom of the air" (Eph. 2:2), the "prince of this world" (John 12:31).

* * * *

By this time we have answered our question: "What is disease as the Bible sees it?" *Disease is just one of the many results of man's sin, along with death, sorrow, guilt, and disasters of nature.*[9] It is part of the general curse from God that the human race must suffer collectively because of its sin.

So what about this curse with its death and disease? Did God merely abandon the world and leave it hopeless? No! Way back in the Book of Genesis He promised that one day a Redeemer would come who would deal both with sin and with sin's results. The whole Old Testament foreshadows this coming One, and as its pages unfold, pictures of this coming Messiah become increasingly clear.

In the first place, the Old Testament makes plain that *the Messiah will deal with sin*. He will do this by forgiving the sins of God's people and by destroying pagan sinners who refuse to obey God.

Secondly, the Old Testament makes plain that *the Messiah will deal with sin's results*. Take the Book of Isaiah for instance. Listen to what it says about how the world of nature will be restored. "For waters shall break forth in the wilderness . . . and the burning sands will become a pool, and the thirsty ground springs of water . . ." (Isa. 35:6-7, RSV). Both the physical earth and the animals will be affected. "The wolf and the lamb shall feed together, the lion shall eat straw like the ox; and dust shall be the serpent's food. They shall not hurt or destroy . . ." (Isa. 65:25, RSV). The ancient prophet foresaw that the sorrow and frustration of mankind would change, and "the ransomed of the Lord . . . shall obtain joy and gladness, and sorrow and sighing shall flee away" (Isa. 35:10, RSV). And as for disease—"Then the eyes of the blind will be opened, and the ears of the deaf will be unstopped. Then the lame will leap like a deer, and the tongue of the dumb will shout for joy" (Isa. 35:5-6).

With promises like these and others, the air of expectation for the Messiah's coming was at fever pitch by Jesus' day.

But there were two misunderstandings held by many who read the Old Testament prophecies. First, many didn't realize that all these good things were to be for the whole world—not just the nation Israel. Secondly, many people—perhaps most—thought that everything the Messiah was to do would be accomplished in a single coming. They didn't understand that their King would come first in humility as a servant, and only later in all His regal splendor. They were right about the fact that the kingdom of God was coming. Their mistake was that they thought it was going to arrive all at once.

In the early portions of the Gospels, a rugged preacher named John the Baptist emerged from the Judean wilderness. From the banks of the Jordan River he called upon the crowds to repent, saying that the kingdom of God was "at hand"—that is, very near (Matt. 3:2).[10] But when Jesus appeared, He announced that the kingdom of God had come.[11] Once, after freeing a demon-possessed man, Jesus said, "If I drive out demons by the Spirit of God, then the kingdom of God *has come* upon you" (Matt. 12:28; Luke 11:20, italics mine). Another time, when some Pharisees asked Jesus, "When will the kingdom of God come?" Jesus gave a surprising reply. "The kingdom of God does not come visibly, nor will people say, 'Here it is,' or 'There it is,' because the kingdom of God is among you"[12] (Luke 17:20-21, NIV—marginal reading).

You see, these Pharisees were expecting the kingdom of God to be an all-at-once affair (Luke 19:11), when God would destroy His enemies and set up His rule in Jerusalem with a spectacular display of divine "fireworks." But what they did not realize was that the King Himself was standing right there in their midst, and because of that, the kingdom of God had in one sense already begun. Though its fullness was still to be in the future,[13] it had already been launched with the coming of Christ. That is why Matthew 4:23 calls the message that Jesus preached "the good news of the kingdom." Jesus had come to challenge Satan's claim as ruler of the earth and to establish His own kingship, claiming back what was rightfully His. He had come to begin to reverse the curse which had followed man's fall into sin. He had come to deal with sin and with sin's results.

How did Jesus deal with sin? He dealt with it by paying its penalty on the cross and by confronting sinful actions and attitudes in people He met.

How did He deal with sin's results? He reversed their effects. Confronted by guilt, Jesus forgave men's sins. Finding disease, He healed the sick. Faced with demon possession, He cast out the spirits by His forceful command. Threatened by the hostilities of nature, He rebuked the storm. "Quiet! Be still!" His amazed disciples breathed a sigh of relief when their boat and their lives were saved, astonished that "even the wind and the waves obeyed Him." Jesus wasn't just proving He can help us through the "storms of life." He was demonstrating His power to reverse the effects of sin upon nature, showing that He was retaking the rule of earth for Himself. It was as if He were saying, "Don't you waves know that I am king here? Satan has ruled this planet long enough, causing you waves to be hostile to man. But I have come to put an end to all of that."

Yes, in dealing with sin and sin's results, Jesus began His kingdom. But underline the word *began* here, for it is so important to the whole question of healing. Jesus put the process in motion, but He didn't finish it then and there. Acts 1:1 refers to the record about Jesus given in the Book of Luke as "all that Jesus *began* to do and to teach" (italics mine).

Sure Jesus cast demons out of people. But He didn't totally wipe out demon possession. Demoniacs still existed after Jesus returned to heaven.

And, yes, Jesus healed the sick. But consider all the people, even in His own country, whom Jesus never met and never healed, let alone those in other parts of the world. And those He did heal grew old and died later on.

Jesus stopped the storm, showing His power over sin's results in the realm of nature. But does that mean all catastrophes of nature were forever erased? Absolutely not.

He raised the dead, and that was wonderful. But there were many godly people whom Jesus did not raise. And even those He raised had to face death again later.

Jesus forgave men's sins—made them righteous in God's eyes. But did He, in their lifetime, free them from the very presence of sin? from having a sinful nature? No. *His purpose wasn't to cement the final brick in His kingdom right then. If He had done that, most of the world would never have had time to hear the Gospel. His plan was to begin the kingdom, to lay the foundation. He wanted to give a foreshadowing of what things would be like at the end of time when the kingdom of God would be a completed building.*

The men who wrote the Epistles stress that we who are Christians are living in two ages at once. We experience the trials, temptations, and problems of this present age, even though we have tasted the powers of the coming age. God is king right now, but He doesn't always "flex His kingly muscles." Rather than totally wiping out sin and its results, He gives Christians a mere taste or "down payment" of what the kingdom in its fullness will be like.

For example, when we get to heaven we will become perfectly righteous and holy. But in the meantime, though we are still sinners, God has given us "the promised Holy Spirit, who is a deposit [or down payment] guaranteeing our inheritance . . ." (Eph. 1:13-14). The way in which the Holy Spirit helps us love God and want to do right in this life is a foretaste of the future when He will make us totally holy and pleasing to God. As a mother gives her children a taste of stew before dinner, so Jesus by His miracles, and the Holy Spirit by His working within us, show us what heaven will be like. But in the meantime, "though inwardly we are being renewed day by day," "outwardly we are wasting away" (2 Cor. 4:16). Though we will one day get the whole package, "meanwhile . . . while we are in this tent [i.e., our bodies], we groan and are burdened" (2 Cor. 5:2-4).

Do you see now why I have sawed through so much theological lumber on this whole subject of sin, sin's results, and the kingdom of God? *Disease is just one of the many results of sin that Jesus began, but didn't finish, dealing with when He started His kingdom while on earth.* Jesus' miracles, including healing, didn't guarantee the end of any of sin's results for those who follow Him.

From time to time God, in His mercy, may grant us healing from disease as a gracious glimpse, a "sneak preview," of what is to come. It is my opinion that He sometimes does. But, in view of the fact that the kingdom has not yet come in its fullness, we are not to automatically expect it. Why should we arbitrarily single out disease—which is just one of sin's many results—and treat it in a special way as something that Christians today shouldn't have to put up with? We are living in "this present age," and the emphasis on earthly trials in the New Testament gives the impression that we're going to have to put up with plenty!

Does Jesus want the best for His children? Sure He does. But that doesn't mean a life of ease and comfort cushioned on a velvet pillow. So when bedsores afflict me as boils did Job, I must say with him, "Shall we indeed accept good from God and not accept adversity?" (Job 2:10). And when I feel bound to my chair as Paul was to his chains, I will say with him, "For it has been granted to you on behalf of Christ not only to believe on him, but also to suffer for him" (Phil. 1:29). I will remember his words:

> "Not only so, but we ourselves, who have the firstfruits of the Spirit, groan inwardly as we wait eagerly for . . . the redemption of our bodies. For in this hope we were saved. But hope that is seen is no hope at all. Who hopes for what he already has? But if we hope for what we do not yet have, we wait for it patiently" (Rom. 8:23-25).

13 Satan Schemes ...God Redeems

Whew! That last chapter covered quite a bit of ground, didn't it? I'll bet some of you are thinking by now, "But what about those four points mentioned back in chapter eleven?"

I haven't forgotten them. But I did want to approach the matter of healing in a general way first. Having sketched a broad background, let's now chalk out answers to the specific points people have written to me about healing as summarized on page 125.

First, what about the idea that since Satan causes disease, and since Jesus came to destroy Satan's work, then Jesus will always heal disease if we ask in faith?

I think this sort of reasoning shows a failure to understand the Bible's teaching on an important subject: the relationship between God and Satan in causing disease (and in causing all calamities, for that matter). The first principle we need to grasp is that *though Satan often causes disease, he can only do what God permits.*

Deep inside, in our less consistent moments, I think we almost unconsciously see the conflict between God and Satan as an arm wrestling match. Their wrists go first this way, then that; God's arm is on top one moment, Satan's the next. God will win in the end (we remind ourselves) because He's slightly stronger and can hold out longer. But it's going to take much time, effort, and a few close calls. It's almost as if we think Satan's schemes throw a monkey wrench into God's plans, catch Him off guard, and present Him with problems He wishes wouldn't happen.

But how silly. The truth is that God is infinitely more powerful than Satan. First John 4:4 tells us, "the one [God] who is in you is greater than the one [Satan] who is in the world." Why, Satan owes his very existence to God. He had to receive God's permission before afflicting Job, and even then was under definite restrictions. His demonic hordes feared Jesus and obeyed Jesus' commands. And the Bible is clear that when our Lord is ready He will crush the Evil One forever.[14]

No, Satan doesn't sneak out and cause pneumonia and cancer while God happens to be looking the other way listening to the prayers of His saints. He can only do what our all-powerful and all-knowing God allows him to do. And we have God's promise that nothing will be allowed which is not for our good or which is too hard for us to bear (Rom. 8:28; 1 Cor. 10:13).

But when we say that God "allows" Satan to do the things he does, I think we sometimes get the wrong idea. It isn't as if Satan twists God's arm and God hesitantly grants, "Well, I guess it'll be okay for you to do such and such . . . but just this once and not too much!" Nor are we to imagine that once God grants permission, He then nervously runs behind Satan with a repair kit, patching up what the devil has ruined, mumbling to Himself, "Now how am I going to work *this* one out for good?" Worse yet is it to suppose that when a Christian becomes ill he has missed "God's best" for him—that the Lord is now forced to go with some divine "Plan B."

No, not only is God not frustrated and hindered by Satan's schemes, but *God actually uses Satan's deeds to serve His own ends and accomplish His own purposes.*

For instance, take the crucifixion of Jesus. Satan clearly played the leading role in instigating the whole thing. He entered the heart of Judas Iscariot, the betrayer of Jesus (John 13:2,26-27). Satan-sponsored evil was working in the hearts of the Jewish mob as they clamored in Jerusalem's streets for the execution of Jesus. Satan-sponsored pride and fear were behind the mock justice handed down by Pilate as he condemned an innocent man in order to gain political popularity. Satan-sponsored sin provoked the cruel soldiers to increase the anguish of the harmless prisoner by torture and ridicule in His last hours of life.

But how did the early Christians, who had God's perspective, view it all? They praised God that the men responsible for Christ's death had only done "what your [God's] power and will had decided beforehand should happen" (Acts 4:28). In his most daring attempt to frustrate the plan of God, Satan cut his own throat and performed the deed which was God's final provision for man's redemption. The world's worst murder became the world's only salvation and dealt the death blow to sin and Satan.

Now suppose God the Father had taken the view many modern Christians take—the view which says: Anything Satan wants must be bad for God's people—the view which implies: If Satan wants one thing to happen, God must want the exact opposite to happen. What would have been the result? Well, God would have stopped Judas from betraying Jesus and stopped the Romans from crucifying Him. In short, He would have canceled the Crucifixion! And if God had canceled the Crucifixion what would have been the result? None of us would be saved!

The truth of the matter is, Satan and God may want the exact same event to take place—but for different reasons. Satan's motive in Jesus' crucifixion was rebellion; God's motive was love and mercy. Satan was a secondary cause behind the Crucifixion, but it was God who ultimately wanted it, willed it, and allowed Satan to carry it out. And the same holds true for disease.

I can imagine someone responding, "But, Joni, how can we possibly say that God is behind disease—that it exists because He wants it to? The Bible tells us that Jesus *healed* disease. Surely that proves God doesn't want it to exist."

Well, let God's own words to Moses speak for themselves—"Then the Lord said to him, 'Who has made man's mouth? Or who makes him dumb or deaf, or seeing or blind? Is it not I, the Lord?'" (Exod. 4:11 NASB). And hear the words of Jeremiah the prophet—"Is it not from the mouth of the Most High that both good and ill go forth?" (Lam. 3:38 NASB). And through Isaiah God says, "I form the light and create darkness, I bring prosperity and create disaster; I, the Lord, do all these things" (Isa. 45:7 NIV).

Does this say God wants disease? I think the key here is how we use the word "want." God doesn't want disease to exist in the sense that He *enjoys* it. He hates it just as He hates all the other results of sin—death, guilt, sorrow, etc. But God must want disease to exist in the sense that He *wills* or *chooses* for it to exist, for if He didn't He would wipe it out immediately.

It's like this. Suppose you were a judge, and a teen-age boy who was caught robbing a store was brought before you. Suppose, too, that the boy's father was your best friend. Would you *enjoy* giving the boy the sentence he deserved? No. Emotionally it would grieve you. But still you would *choose* to sentence him, for that would be the moral and just thing to do.

So God chooses to allow sickness—for many reasons. One of them is in order to mold Christian character. In this way God uses one form of evil (sickness) to help remove another form of evil (personal sin). And there are other reasons, too. The benefits mentioned earlier in this book applying to other trials apply to disease as well. But perhaps the most comforting reason was mentioned in the last chapter. God is delaying closing the curtain on sin and its results until more of the world can have the chance to hear the gospel. For if God erased all disease today, He would also have to erase sin, the cause of disease, and that would mean the destruction of all sinners. It is God's *mercy* which delays His judgment on disease and sin.

But I can imagine another objection some may raise to the way I have viewed God's relationship to disease in this chapter. It has to do with Satan. Is it true that God grants permission for Satan to spread disease? "Since everything Satan does stems from sinful rebellion," some reason, "then to say God allows Satan to act sinful and cause disease makes God a sinner."

That's a tough objection to handle, and I certainly don't understand everything about God's relationship to Satan. But the Bible does make two things absolutely clear: On the one hand, God sovereignly controls even Satan's actions. On the other hand, God is in no way a sinner nor the author of sin![15]

When the Bible presents us with two truths like these which seem opposed to one another, how are we to handle them? How can we fit them together? The easy way out is to deny one side or the other. (In this case that usually means denying God's sovereignty.) But that's wrong. What we should do is first be sure that both truths are really what the Bible is teaching. Once we're sure of that, we must humbly bow our reason to the authority of God's Word, accepting both truths in faith. When God tells us something we're to believe Him, even if what He says seems paradoxical to our finite minds.

The best illustration of this I can think of is the doctrine of the Trinity. Scripture plainly says there is but one God. Yet it also plainly teaches that the Father, Son, and Holy Spirit are each God although they are three distinct persons. No true Christian denies any of these truths even though human reason can't fit them together. Why should we treat the biblical truths about God's sinless nature and yet His sovereign control over Satan any differently?

Satan, as king of this world, has been granted the power to wreak havoc and disaster. He does so because he is going to hell, and misery loves company. He sends disease and trouble because he hates mankind and he hates God. But God exploits Satan's evil intentions and uses them in His own service—just one more example of His ability to work "out everything in conformity with the purpose of his will" (Eph. 1:11).

Satan intends the rain which ruins a church picnic to cause the people to curse their Lord; but God uses the rain to develop their patience. Satan plans to hinder the work of an effective missionary by arranging for him to trip and break a leg; God allows the accident so that the missionary's patient response to the pain and discomfort will bring glory to Himself. Satan brews a hurricane to kill thousands in a small Indian village so he can enjoy the misery and destruction; God uses the storm to display His awesome power, to show people the awful consequences that sin has brought to the world, to drive some to search for Him, to harden others in their sin, and to remind us that He is free to do as He pleases—that we will never figure Him out. Satan schemed that a seventeen-year-old girl named Joni would break her neck, hoping to ruin her life; God sent the broken neck in answer to her prayer for a closer walk with Him and uses her wheelchair as a platform to display His sustaining grace.

As a friend once said, "God sends things, but Satan often brings them." Praise God that when Satan causes us illness—or any calamity—we can answer him with the words Joseph answered his brothers who sold him into slavery, "As for you, you meant evil against me, but God meant it for good" (Gen. 50:20).

* * * *

So much for the relationship between Satan and sickness. Let's move on to the second point people have written to me regarding miraculous healing (remember? back on page 125). The point was: because Jesus Christ is "the same yesterday, today, and forever" and because in the Gospels He healed all who came to Him in faith, mustn't He do the same today? This subject came up some time after the healing service in the little oak church.

It was one of those cold winter evenings when Steve and I were sitting by the fireplace. Some of my family were in the kitchen dressing warmly to go out in the falling snow. Steve caught that longing look on my face as I stared at my sisters while they bundled up in their scarves and coats.

"You'd really like to go out there with them, wouldn't you?" he said.

Startled, I answered, "Oh, no, I don't . . ." But I paused, then continued, "Well, yeah, I guess it *would* be nice to be on my feet. You know, Steve, it's been more than a year since that healing service at the church."

Steve, sensing I wanted to get into something heavy, pulled his chair closer.

"Look," I questioned, "do you know of any place in the Bible where it says that Jesus turned down someone who wanted to be healed?"

He thought a moment with a contemplative wrinkling of his forehead. "No, I can't think of any," and shook his head.

"Then you believe the Bible when it says in the Gospels that Jesus healed those who were brought to Him, right?"

"Oh, certainly," he replied and reached for his Bible on the table.

"And God's Word says that Jesus Christ is 'the same yesterday, today, and forever,' doesn't it?"

"It sure does."

"It also says that God never changes, right?"

"Right."

"Then if Jesus healed all those who came to Him in faith, and if He never changes, won't He surely heal all those who come to Him in faith today?"

Steve stood up and started slowly walking around the table. He took a deep breath, paused to collect his throughts, and then responded, weighing his words. "Joni, your logic sounds inescapable. Jesus did heal those who asked Him back then. And He doesn't ever change. But to conclude that He has to act in the same way today—I've got to answer 'no.'"

Seeing the "why?" written on my face, he began to explain himself. "I think the basic mistake in that line of reasoning comes from failing to distinguish between *who God is* and *what He does*. Who He is never changes, but what He does often will."

He went on to explain that God's character and attributes are the things about Him that cannot change. For instance, He could never become more holy than He is now, or more loving, or more faithful. Neither could He become less of any of these. That's because God is already perfect in all His traits, and for Him to change in any way would mean a move toward imperfection.

Allowing time for that to sink in, he walked over to the hearth to place a log on the fire. "Here, let me make it clear. It's like a person standing at the North Pole," he suggested, talking with his hands in typical Steve fashion. "When you're there, you're as far north as you can go. Move one step in any direction, and you've moved south."

I asked, "You mean if God were to change, He wouldn't be God any more?"

"Exactly," he confirmed, slapping his hand to his side. "When you're at the top, if you're going to move, there's no place to go but down. And because God's character and traits are 'at the top,' they're never going to change—or as the Bible puts it, 'He's the same yesterday, today, and forever.'"

Steve continued, "But that's not to put God into a box and say that He can't act. It's wrong to picture God as a meditating mystic who sits motionless for hours and doesn't even budge to swat a fly from his nose. The Bible is full of God's acts, and any act involves change."

"Not change in His character," I echoed, "but a change in what He does." Things were beginning to fit together, and my face brightened as Steve agreed.

He elaborated on the fact that God has a plan for the human race and that history is constantly moving toward a climactic goal. At one time God acted through a nation; now He acts through His church.

Once Jesus submitted to those who mocked Him; someday He will take vengeance on His enemies. What is fitting at one time in His plan is not fitting at another. The God whose character is never-changing is directing a grand play where the props and lines are constantly changing, ever moving toward the final scene and the closing of the curtain.

Glancing out the window at my sisters returning with their sleds, I mused, "Then in answer to my question, are you saying that miracles of healing aren't fitting for today?"

"Joni, we just can't generalize about that. It may be good for God to heal one person and not another, or even to heal a person at one time in his life and not at another time. I believe that God sometimes still heals miraculously today when people pray. But I do think that miracles had a *special* place for the days of Christ and His apostles." He wheeled me away from the window and pushed me to the table.

Sitting down beside me, he opened up his Bible and went on to explain. I learned how miracles had a special place *for the time of Christ* because they proved He was who He claimed to be—Israel's Messiah. They showed that His kingdom had the power to reverse the awful effects of sin, such as death and disease.

Miracles had a special place *for the time of the apostles* because they proved that the apostles, too, were who they claimed to be—Christ's specially chosen men to get the wobbly-kneed, newborn church on its feet. The Book of Acts (where we read about the apostles and all they did) is the record of a unique time in the history of God's people—a unique time with unique problems. Thus, they needed special leaders such as the apostles.

In the first place, there had never been any Christian missionaries before. Yet Christ had told His followers to spread the gospel to the whole earth. What a task! And so God assisted the early church's first splash into an icy cold world by giving them leaders who could do miraculous deeds. Acts 2:43 tells us that "Everyone was filled with awe, and many wonders and miracles were done by the apostles."

Another unique problem the early church had was the confusion that so many new Christians felt who had been raised in Judaism. Steve asked me to imagine myself as the father of a Jewish family recently turned Christian, living in Palestine early in the first century.

"Picture this, Joni," he grinned. "For centuries your people have faithfully followed Jewish law regarding offering sacrifices, circumcising all males, not eating certain meats, and not associating with Gentiles. Naturally, the old way of life lingers on. After all, you *are* still a Jew. One day your best friend, also a Christian Jew (but acting a bit strange lately), springs some news on you.

> "Hey, old buddy, did you hear?"
>
> "Hear what?"
>
> "About the big change. Since God's Son has died on the cross as the final sacrifice for sin, we don't have to offer animals at the temple any more."
>
> Flinging your arms up, you exclaim in amazement, "Are you out of your mind?! Not offer sacrifices? I mean, I believe in Jesus, but we've *always* offered sacrifices."
>
> "And that's not all," he continues excitedly. "We don't have to circumcise our sons any more."
>
> "Not circumcise our boys! Why . . . (cough!) . . . that's . . . (sputter!) . . . how can you. . ."
>
> "And there's more—we can eat any meats we

want to. And we're supposed to love all Gentiles as if they were our brothers! In fact, I'm inviting you and old Flavius Marcus over for pork dinner tonight."

"*Me* eat pork?!" Holding your hands to your head, you run out screaming, "With Flavius, the pig herder?!!"

I laughed as Steve finished his story. "Well," he concluded, "you can imagine the difficulties that arose between Jewish and Gentile Christians. There needed to be some respected and capable leaders, such as the apostles, who could take charge and settle disputes."

He went on to tell how there was something else that made the apostolic age a special time. There was no New Testament as such yet, and the teachings of Jesus might easily be forgotten or distorted. Though the Holy Spirit was giving some Christians prophecies and revelations to fill in as stop-gaps until the full New Testament message could be written down and made permanent, there were many impostors. False teachers, hungry to feed their own egos, lurked behind every tree, waiting like wolves to pounce on God's flock and lead them into error. Since there was no New Testament to appeal to as an absolute standard by which to measure truth, the apostles were God's men to "ride herd" over the situation and authoritatively guard the church from error.

Yet with all the phony apostles running around, how were the real apostles of Christ to prove themselves genuine? Paul answers that question in his letters to the Corinthian church. He claims they can know he is for real because of his consistent life and the success of his ministry with them.[16] But his final defense is found in 2 Corinthians 12:12. "The things that mark an apostle—signs, wonders and miracles

—were done among you with great perseverance." *Miracles had the definite purpose of spotlighting those men whom God had appointed to begin and lead His church.* God also added weight to the apostles' authority by the fact that, in addition to doing miracles themselves, others received miraculous gifts under their ministry. Apparently this did not happen under the ministry of non-apostles.[17]

"Special men for a special time," Steve summarized. "That's what the apostles were. In fact, they were so special that Ephesians 2:20 tells us the whole church was built upon the foundation of the apostles and New Testament prophets, with Jesus Himself as the chief cornerstone. Now that's quite a rank and honor, a position not given to the rest of us.

"Look at all those books about healing up on your shelf," Steve pointed up above my desk. Taking one down, he said, "I've read this one myself. Let me show you something in here." He flipped through the pages.

"See, here the author quotes Jesus' words to the Twelve in Matthew 10:8—'Heal the sick, raise the dead, cleanse those who have leprosy, drive out demons. Freely you have received, freely give.'" His finger moved down the page to the next paragraph.

"Down here he uses that verse to say we should be out doing the same. Joni, if Jesus' words there apply directly to us, it means we should all be out raising the dead!

"One more thing," he concluded. "No matter what we believe as to how important miracles were for then as opposed to now, one thing is certain: we can't point to what God did yesterday as proof that He's got to do the same thing today. If that were true, He'd have to keep our shoes and clothes from wearing out today because He did it for the Israelites as they wandered in the wilderness!"[18]

It began making sense to me. Although we can learn much from reading about the apostles, that doesn't necessarily mean we can do everything they did. God sent them to help the church at a time when they were desperately needed. Instead of getting frustrated and jealous because we can't do everything the apostles did, we should be praising God's wisdom in giving them special gifts appropriate to their situation and in giving us special grace appropriate to ours.

Neither Steve nor I had kept track of the hours as they had slipped by. The snow had stopped, the fire had died, and it was long past the time when I should have been in bed. Steve yawned, stretched, and got up to leave.

Picking up our empty Coke bottles, he hesitated a minute and then said, "Jon, this talk hasn't been easy for me. I've really had to wrestle with these things watching you these years in that wheelchair. If there's anyone anywhere who'd love to see you walk, it's me."

"I know that," I assured him.

I don't want you to just blindly accept everything I've told you tonight. I'm just asking you to give it some prayerful thought with an open mind."

And that's all I'm asking you, the reader, to do.

14 Prayers And Promises

But the verses we read in that little oak church seemed so clear! I'm talking about all those Bible promises which seem to guarantee Christians that *all* their prayers will be answered, including prayers for healing. Remember?

> "I will do whatever you ask in my name, so that the Son may bring glory to the Father. You may ask me for anything in my name, and I will do it" (John 14:13-14). —Jesus

> "I tell you the truth, if anyone says to this mountain, 'Go, throw yourself into the sea,' and does not doubt in his heart but believes that what he says will happen, it will be done for him. Therefore I tell you, whatever you ask in prayer, believe that you will receive it, and it will be yours" (Mark 11:23-24). —Jesus

> "I can do everything through him who gives me strength" (Phil. 4:13). —Paul

And this brings us to the third and fourth points in chapter eleven: We have promises in Scripture that whatever we ask in Jesus' name will be done for us—including health and healing.

These are staggering promises, but they pose a problem. I mean, when's the last time you actually saw a mountain throw itself into the sea? Godly Christians pray in faith and in Jesus' name for a lot of things that never happen. So when Christians don't get their prayers answered (that is, when God's answer is "no"), what are we to do with verses like these? We can't just avoid them or attempt to make them mean something we'd feel comfortable with. Yet to put these verses by themselves on a plaque over our fireplace and then view them as God's word-for-word promise that all our prayers will be answered our way can really bring frustration. I'll be the first to admit that I've sometimes felt as though my prayers just bounced off the ceiling and never got through. Haven't you felt the same way?

Now I don't know all the reasons why God says yes to some prayers and not others. And I don't know the complete meaning of all these verses. But I've found it a real help to compare different sections of Scripture and let one throw light upon another. And you know what? God sure does guarantee answers to prayer. When Jesus gave His disciples these promises, He was saying, "Look, I'm giving you a job to do, and I promise you'll have everything you need to get it done. If there's a mountain in your way, ask Me and I'll mow it down." And those apostles did see mountains move as they changed the course of history!

But I also found that God gave two conditions which must be met if our prayers are to be guaranteed answers: we must be living in close fellowship with Him, and our requests must be in line with His will.

Fellowship With God

When I was a high school student, I, like many Christians, tended to think of myself as the center of life rather than God. Oh, I was trusting Christ as my Savior from sin, and I more or less tried to do what was right. But the basic thing on my mind when I thought about God was, "What can He do for *me?* How can serving Christ give *me* joy? How do *I* feel at the end of a worship service?" Naturally, this "God-exists-to-make-me-happy" mentality carried over into my prayer life. Forgetting that God expects and demands holiness from His children, I reasoned, "If God wants only the best for me, then surely He will answer my prayers, even if I don't exactly live like an angel."

But I was in for a rude awakening. Leafing through the Psalms during devotions one day, I stumbled upon this verse: "If I regard wickedness in my heart, the Lord will not hear" (Ps. 66:18). *Gulp! How can that be? I thought God listened to everybody.* But over the years I found other verses which said the same thing. James 5:16 says that the prayer of a righteous man is powerful and effective. *Oh, I don't need to worry about that,* I consoled myself. *Since I'm a Christian, I'm righteous in God's eyes no matter how I live.* But someone pointed out to me that all through his book James isn't talking about the *legal* righteousness God gives us, but the *obedient* righteousness we give Him. In other words, if I wanted God to hear me, I'd better start listening to Him.

Peter adds his voice to James' by cautioning husbands to treat their wives with respect. He goes on to tell them why—"so that nothing will hinder your prayers" (1 Peter 3:7). Remember that Peter was standing right there when Jesus gave all those astounding promises in the Gospels. Yet he didn't take Jesus to mean, "Prayer is like a blank check. Just fill in the amount whenever you like, no matter what your spiritual condition, and I'll cash it for you." No, God only guarantees that faithful Christians who "telephone" Him get through immediately. Backslidden believers might expect a busy signal unless they're calling to say, "Forgive me. I'm sorry."

Jesus Himself, who gave these promises, qualified what He meant in John 15:7. *"If you remain in me and my words remain in you,* ask whatever you wish, and it will be given you" (italics mine). When he says "remain in me," He's talking about a consistent life style of closeness to Him, not a sporadic spirituality.

When I was in high school, we ran several weeks of cross-country in gym class every fall. When the whistle blew, most of us started out at a relaxed pace, and soon the majority of girls found the pace they knew they could keep up for the whole distance. But there were always a few who shot off sprinting like a kid who had just hit a baseball through the neighbor's window. Before most of us had made the bend, they were half-way around the field. Pretty soon we would pass them as they slowed down to catch their breath. Then they'd zoom by us again, only to fall behind the second time. At the end of the race the steady, consistent runners always did the best.

In the same way, when we dash off with a sudden surge of spiritual zeal, that doesn't necessarily mean we are "remaining in Christ." Sudden zeal isn't bad, but it may be deceptive. As I know from personal experience, we can be "super-Christian" one week and a discouraged quitter the next. Now, God promises to answer the prayers of those who maintain a steady walk with Him, and that involves some maturity. Of course, all Christians will have their ups and downs, so I'm not talking about perfection. The very best Christian falls infinitely short of that. And because God is so gracious, at times He may hear us even when we are out of fellowship with Him. But the more consistent our life with Christ becomes, the more we can expect our prayers to be answered.

Jesus wasn't speaking in general terms when He told us to remain in Him. He got specific by adding the phrase, "and [if] my words remain in you." This refers to more than just the actual words He said while on earth, the words printed in red in some Bibles. He meant the Bible in general, for Christ's Spirit inspired all the Scriptures. To have Christ's words remain in you does not mean you have to get a seminary degree or Bible school diploma. Nor does it require memorizing "grocery lists" of biblical names and places so you can win a game of Bible Trivia when someone tries to stump you with "Who was Zechariah's mother-in-law?" You can know tons of Bible and theology without ever letting it grip your soul. I think Jesus was referring to running Scripture through your mind over and over again in order to find new ways to please God and bring Him praise. Like David's attitude when he wrote, "Thy word I have treasured in my heart, that I may not sin against Thee" (Ps. 119:11).

So there we have it. To get our prayers answered we need to walk with God and be in His Word. But I fear that too many of us want the power of Paul's prayers without the discipline of Paul's life. At one time or another we've all been guilty of approaching God as though He's some great spiritual Vending Machine in the sky—drop in a prayer and out comes the answer. But God isn't a machine; He's a person.

My sister Kathy can feel free to ask my sister Jay, "May I borrow your car tonight?" because Kathy is close to Jay, loves her, treats her well, and has cultivated a relationship with her. But if you're a supposed "friend" of Jay who hasn't even called for two years, don't expect to casually drop by one day, turn on the old charm, and con her into loaning you her car.

Human relationships don't work that way. Neither

do relationships with God. We can't expect Him to hear our prayers if we only come running to Him when we want something or get into trouble. And even when we're living close to Him, we have no license to expect "healing upon demand" or anything else upon demand. Because we exist to serve God, not vice versa, we're to humbly request things from Him, remembering who He is. Then, as the apostle John says, we will "receive from him anything we ask," not because we demand it, but "because we obey his commands and do what pleases him" (1 John 3:22).

God's Will

But what if you're a Christian who is really trying to remain in Christ and yet you're sick? Perhaps it's a head cold. Perhaps it's leukemia. But after four healing services and countless prayers and tears, you're still sick. What's wrong? Maybe you could relate when I shared my own experience of not getting healed because you, too, feel guilty that nothing's happened. Perhaps you've searched your heart for any hidden sins until you'd almost invent some so you could confess them and be healed. It could be that certain pages in your Bible are over-worn from where you've underlined different promises in ink and have read those promises aloud to God. But though you've rung heaven's phones off the hook and have promised God you'll do anything if only He heals you, all you get is silence.

If this is your situation, you are not alone; thousands of other Christians are just like you. And my heart goes out to you because I know exactly what it feels like to have well-meaning Christians give subtle hints that my condition is self-imposed.

But after looking everywhere else for the reason why my prayers for healing weren't answered, I was forced to return to God's Word and take a closer look. It was there I found something which shed light not only on my questions about divine healing, but on the whole issue of why Christians suffer. It's such a simple thing. If you have tried everything to be healed but nothing has changed, then *has it ever really hit you that the reason you are in your present condition is that God, in His wisdom, wills it to be so?*

You see, the same apostle John who recorded God's promise that whatever we ask in Jesus' name will come true (John 14:13) also said that God puts a condition on that promise. In 1 John 5:14 he tells us, "We have this assurance in approaching God, that if we ask anything *according to his will,* He hears us" (italics mine). Now that's quite an "if." Not . . . if we ask anything we think we might like . . . or anything that would make life easier . . . or even anything that we imagine God would want . . . but anything that's actually "according to His will." For God to answer our prayers, they must be in line with His will.

But why in the world would it possibly be God's will to deny a Christian's request for healing? In some ways, this whole book is about that very thing. The pages of Scripture teem with good things that can come from suffering. Pain and discomfort get our minds off the temporary things of this world and force us to think about God. They drive us to pull His Word off the shelf far more than usual and to pay more attention when we do. Trials knock us off our proud pedestals and get us relying on God (2 Cor. 1:9). Then we learn to know God better, for when we have to depend on someone to get us through each hour, we really get to know them. Problems give us the chance to praise God even when it's hard. This pleases Him and proves to the spirit world how great He is to inspire such loyalty. And it proves something to us—it gives us a gauge to measure the depth or shallowness of our own commitment to Him.

Sometimes sickness serves as God's chastiser to wake us from our sin (1 Cor. 11:29-30; 1 Peter 4:1). This proves to us that He loves us, for every good father disciplines his children (Heb. 12:5-6). Sometimes God uses suffering to help us relate to others who are suffering (2 Cor. 1:3-4). And the list could go on. If nothing else, the fact that while Jesus was on earth God matured Him through suffering should tell us something (Heb. 2:10). It should make us ask ourselves the question, "Should I expect anything less?

I sometimes shudder to think where I would be today if I had not broken my neck. I couldn't see at first why God would possibly allow it, but I sure do now. He has gotten so much more glory through my paralysis than through my health! And believe me, you'll never know how rich that makes me feel. If God chooses to heal you in answer to your prayers, that's great. Thank Him for it. But if He chooses not to, thank Him anyway. You can be sure He has His reasons.

I can hear someone saying, "Joni, if we think that way, if we don't expect God to heal us, He won't! Ending a prayer for healing with the words 'If it be Thy will' actually shows a lack of faith. Shouldn't we strive to reach the place where we're so in touch with God that we can just sort of sense what He wills in every case and then pray with full faith and assurance?" But what a contrast this view is to the biblical picture of our God! He is so above us that we will never figure Him out: "O the depth of the riches, the wisdom and the knowledge of God! How unsearchable his judgments and his paths beyond tracing out! Who has known the mind of the Lord? Or who has been his adviser?" (Rom. 11:33-34).

The authors of the New Testament didn't claim

to always know God's mind. James tells us we shouldn't say, "Tomorrow I'm going to go to such and such a place and do so and so." Rather, our attitude should be, "If it is the Lord's will, we will live and do this or that" (James 4:15). Once when Paul was asked by some Christians to stay in Ephesus to help teach them, he didn't pretend to be able to read God's mind, but merely said, "I will come back if it is God's will" (Acts 18:21).

One of the main reasons we need to pray with an "if-it-be-Thy-will" attitude is that it's so easy for us to make mistakes and misread God's will. Countless times I have fooled myself into believing the prayers I prayed were for God's glory when actually they were for myself. "God, don't let me make a fool of myself when I give my talk in speech class. If I do, the kids will think that all Christians are weirdos, and that'll hurt Your reputation." Now if that's what I had actually meant, my prayer would have been okay. But deep inside, I think what was really on my mind was, "God, don't let me flop this talk because I don't want to have my bubble burst." Maybe God knew that what was *really* hurting His reputation was my self-centered attitude at school and that a lousy speech would serve His purpose better than answering my prayer.

But our motives don't need to be selfish or sinful in order for us to misread God's plan. We can make honest mistakes.[19] Let me give you an example.

One afternoon about a year ago a nice-looking, dark-haired young man in his mid-twenties, whom I had never met before, appeared at our door asking to see me. My sister Jay invited him in and left the two of us to talk in the den. During the awkward conversation which followed, I learned he had driven all the way from his home in the Southwest just to meet me. Obviously nervous, he said God had revealed to him that I was to become his wife and that he should propose to me. In his mind, it was clearly God's will that we be married. He became very unsettled when I told him that, strangely enough, he was about the tenth such person in the past two years whom "God had told" to propose to me. Had God misled him? Had He misled the other nine?

No, we concluded after discussing it for a while. God is not a God of confusion. He doesn't mis*lead* us; we mis*read* Him. Then we went on to talk about some "safer" ways to discover God's will—like applying principles from His Word, getting the advice of mature Christians, and waiting to see which doors God opens and closes. By the time the young man left, he was much more at ease. Convinced God hadn't played a joke on him, he drove away feeling that the things he had learned had made his trip worthwhile.

It takes real humility and self-denial to put our pleas for healing before God and then willingly leave the answer with Him. Jesus so beautifully illustrated this in His prayer of anguish in Gethsemane. In His personal desire He desperately wished to avoid the horrors of the cross, saying, "Father, if you are willing, take this cup from me"; but His last clause made possible the salvation of mankind—"yet not my will, but yours be done" (Luke 22:42). Surely, at least part of what it means to pray "in Jesus' name" is to pray in the same spirit in which He prayed in His darkest hour—giving God our requests but leaving the results with Him.

Look How Far We've Come—A Summary

Jesus gave wonderful promises to His disciples; whatever they needed to get God's work done on earth, He would give. But Jesus' own words and the rest of Scripture make it clear that there were at least two conditions to any prayer they made—they must be remaining in Him, and their request must be in line with God's will. Since God hasn't chosen to reveal all of His will to Christians, then we must leave our requests in His hands and wait to see what He decides to do. And if He chooses to refuse our request? Well, there is more than one way to "move a mountain." The New Testament stresses that God loves to use weak vessels (people) to do His work so that He, and not they, gets the glory. And in light of all the spiritual benefits resulting from sickness and suffering, God may choose that our very sickness be His way of moving the mountains before us.

As we grow in our faith, our way of looking at things changes. Once it seemed as if the only way God could glorify Himself would be to *remove* our sufferings. Now it becomes clear that He can glorify Himself *through* our sufferings.

As for healings and other miracles of God—just because they had a *special* place for the days of Christ and His apostles doesn't mean they have *no* place for today. In reacting to the "God wants to heal everybody" extreme, many of us have over-reacted and joined the "God never wants to heal anybody" extreme. In this case, what we mistakenly call "unemotionalism" in reality is probably plain unbelief. We do not have because we do not ask.

But that's not to say that any time we ask in faith for healing God is obligated to give it to us. Even in apostolic times godly Christians sometimes had to endure illness. During his travels, the apostle Paul, whom God used to heal many, had to leave his friend Trophimus sick in Miletus (2 Tim. 4:20). In 1 Timothy 5:23 Paul urged his friend Timothy to "use a little wine because of your stomach and frequent illnesses." He didn't say, "Pray more about it," or "Come and see me about it." He said, "Take something for it." Christians are to pray for healing, but they are not necessarily to think something is wrong if God refuses the request.

Finally, we should not deceive ourselves into believing that miracles are the ultimate weapon to convince a sinful world. At the end of Jesus' own life, though He had done all kinds of miracles, some men jeered, "If you're really the Messiah, come down off that cross and then we'll believe." Before going to the cross, Jesus confided to His disciples that their generation was especially guilty because they had seen so many wonders and still, on the whole, didn't believe (John 15:24). No, we can be certain that if a man's heart is hardened in sin against God, even the most spectacular divine sign won't change his mind, unless the Holy Spirit opens his eyes.

Do you remember the book that fell off my desk several chapters ago? Well, I still can't pick it up. It sure would be nice to have the use of my hands again so I could reach it. But the wish is fading. For my paralysis has drawn me close to God and given a spiritual healing which I wouldn't trade for a hundred active years on my feet.

WHEN THE PIECES DON'T SEEM TO FIT

15 Let God Be God

During my first year in the hospital I would sometimes leaf through my Bible using a mouthstick. I suppose I learned some things, but reading was mainly a pastime—on par with watching soap operas and listening to the radio. Not until I got home did I give God's Word any kind of serious study. When I did, it made the difference between night and day. Seeing things through God's eyes instead of my own helped me to begin fitting together the puzzle pieces of my suffering. I was getting a taste of genuine wisdom. *Maybe if I keep at it,* I reasoned, *one day I'll be fully wise—able to understand ALL of God's purposes in EVERYTHING that happens.*

But as my Christian life progressed, things didn't work out that way. Often I could see how some specific trial was working out for my good. But sometimes I couldn't. For instance, I knew that trials are sent to build us up. But there were days when the problems were piled on so high they only seemed to wear me down—even when I took them as from God. *The Lord promises that days like this will turn out for my good,* I thought, *but HOW? I just can't see it!*

And that wasn't all. In addition to my own unsettling experiences, I began learning about others who endured trials for which I had no answers. People began writing me with problems I just couldn't understand, even with an open Bible. Oh, sure, in one sense I could understand. I knew the various explanations in Scripture for why God lets us suffer. But matching up which explanation fits each particular trial was another story. What would you have said to the young girl who wrote this letter?

> Dear Joni,
>
> . . . My father died when I was two years old and my mother has been very ill with cancer for a year now. . . . I am trying to understand why God allowed this to happen. Sometimes I spend a lot of time just wondering what it will be like when Mom dies and I am alone. I have been trying to get closer to God so I will not be bitter when this happens. I have already received Jesus as my Lord and Savior, but the depression I have from watching Mom suffer causes me to have a hard time concentrating long enough to read and study His Word. Just sitting around watching TV and sleeping seems to be all I can handle.

I could give this girl some helpful advice as to how to respond to her problems in a God-honoring way. But give her the specific "Why" behind her troubles? That was a different story. Was God's purpose in her trials to make her more like Christ or to get her thoughts on spiritual things? To make her an example to the angelic world or to give her the ability to comfort others? I might guess, but I didn't know. Whatever God's reason, at least on the surface it didn't seem to be working.

In fact, some of the trials people wrote to me about actually seemed to *hurt* God's cause.

> Dear Joni,
>
> Please understand as I write this that I am not feeling sorry for myself and I am not an atheist. I thought

that after I read your story I would be finally able to see things differently. But though I admire you if you honestly believe the way you do, I still have just not been able to understand the cruel things in your life and in the life of my brother.

My brother is 26 years old and has been a Quad [i.e., paralyzed in four limbs] since 1965 due to an auto accident. . . . Like you he had quite a bit going for him at the time of his accident. Being a Quad yourself you know what he went through.

He finally made up his mind to do something with the only thing he had left—his mind. He studied Psychology at home, went to work as an aide for the Governor of Indiana and was going to go to college in Ohio for more Psychology. He lost his job after only two weeks because Medicaid could not pay his medical bills if he was working. He *wanted* to work, he didn't want to be dependent on other people, and like you he *didn't* want pity.

I talk in the past tense because my brother is now in a nursing home in a comatose state as of October 1976 due to a freak accident. He lived like a normal person the way he *wanted* to, and he kept his mind alert at all times. Now, Someone has decided to take his mind away. If you feel that's fair or that there's a reason for that, please help me understand it.

Any explanations I might have sent to this young man would probably come off sounding like hollow little formulas—trite clichés. And to be honest, they probably wouldn't have satisfied me deep down inside either. Sometimes the magnitude of a person's problems seems to outweigh any potential benefit which might come as a result. I felt that way when I read this woman's letter.

Dear Joni,

I am a 22-year-old triplegia (paralyzed in three limbs). This happened to me in 1968 after my mother hit me on the head. It took six surgeries to save me. I was at Cook County Hospital for one year. Then I was sent to the Rehabilitation Institute of Chicago for a year and a half. Then I went to Grant Hospital for surgery on my arms and legs.

I have been back to the Rehabilitation Institute eight times. So far I have had 22 surgeries. I am still the same. I am in a chair. I have no family and I take care of myself. I have read your book and would like to know how to cope with depression. I don't have a lot of faith in God. I feel I cannot overcome this. Please tell me how you feel about this.

I began to wonder, "Will I ever become truly wise and be able to understand God's mind in all of this?" My friend Steve didn't help matters any when he told me about the experiences of his cousin, a young woman who until recently lived not far from me. She shares those experiences here:

When my mom was only sixteen, a local alcoholic a few years older than she said he'd kill her parents if she wouldn't marry him, so she did. He was like a maniac and used to beat her black and blue when he was drunk. We grew up extremely poor on a farm in Tennessee, and mom had to work hard in the fields to keep food on the table. . . . I remember once mom gathering us kids and running to the hills behind our house. I thought the reason dad was chasing us with the gun was that he was only playing cowboys and Indians (I was so little). But when I saw the fear in mom's face, I knew it was for real. Later that night we sneaked back to the house when dad fell asleep drunk and it was safe. . . . One time when he was drunk he lined us all up against the wall, pointed a loaded gun, and said he was going to kill us one by one and then kill himself. If a neighbor hadn't happened to drop by and then help us, I guess we'd be dead. Dad drowned when I was seven.

Even after mom remarried and we moved north, trouble seemed to follow us. Mom had a gun pulled on her up here. And two years ago when she worked in a store three robbers tied and gagged her, locked her in

> the ladies' room, and put a knife to her throat. They said they'd kill her if she screamed. . . .
>
> She's spent the last nine weeks in the hospital with raynauds disease. It turns your hands and toes dark black and hurts like frostbite wearing off. She hasn't had a good night's sleep the entire time from the pain—pain so bad she can't even stand to have the sheet touch her fingers. When her left foot got gangrene, they thought they might have to amputate, but they were able to save it. . . . Three fingers on her left hand had to go, though, down to the first joint. We all keep trusting the Lord, but it sure gets hard sometimes.

Could even the most mature Christian fully explain God's reasoning in all of this? But that wasn't all! Steve's cousin went on to tell of her stepfather's serious health problems and surgeries, the crushed shoulder her brother received in a car accident that left his right arm immobilized, and her own operations for cancer. But the last episode she shared was the must unbelievable. It took place on her farm early one morning in August of 1975:

> I had seen my husband, Buddy, and the kids off for the day. After getting dressed for work, I came downstairs to go out through the kitchen door to my car. When I got to the kitchen I was startled to see a man there, leaning over the washer. But when he turned my way I recognized him as the teen-age boy from the farm a quarter mile up the road. "What are you doing here?" I asked, thinking it strange that he hadn't knocked. Usually the dogs bark at a stranger, but they hadn't today. But he didn't say a word, just sort of stared with a kind of dazed look. Then he showed a knife in his hand and began walking towards me.
>
> I backed up and started to scream, but he kept coming. Finally he stopped right in front of me and then stabbed his knife into my right side. When I felt the hot liquid pouring out, I put my hand over the wound to keep from losing too much blood. But it

didn't do any good, because he started stabbing me all over. All the while I kept screaming, "Why?! Why?!" When I went for a kitchen knife to defend myself, the drawer just came out and fell to the floor. I think the scariest thing was when I saw my own blood all over the floor. I slumped to the floor, and after what seemed like ages he finally left.

After he had gone I got hold of myself and then began faltering over to the phone to call for help. It wasn't until I heard the kitchen door open behind me that I realized he had never really left, but had waited outside to see what I'd do. My heart sank, and I knew I'd never make it to the phone. "I'm going to kill you this time," he said very matter-of-factly. Then he raised his knife and started stabbing me all over again. After slashing my wrist and behind my knee he pricked his knife in my stomach over and over. It was more awful than I can describe.

He asked me if my husband was home, and I said, "Yes, and he's coming downstairs!" But when nobody came he knew I had lied and came at me again. I managed to yell, "You've already killed me. Why don't you just leave me alone!" Then just as calm as anything he wiped his mouth with his sleeve and turned and left.

I was getting weaker and weaker as I lost more blood, but I knew I'd have to wait until he left for good before trying anything this time. When I was almost ready to black out, I know it was God who gave me the strength to get to my feet and stumble to the phone. I pushed the "0" button and had just enough time to tell the operator the bare essentials before a black curtain fell and I was out.

They tell me that it was two days before they knew if I'd live or not. It took somewhere around fifty stitches all over my body. I had to have my spleen removed, and they had to repair my liver, pancreas, and collapsed lung.

Steve tells me that after serving only one month in a minimum security detention home the attacker was transferred to a mental institution and was allowed home on weekends. Fourteen months later he was freed. Although God has given Steve's cousin remarkable ability to forgive her assailant and not be bitter, after three years she still feels the effects. In order to go to the bathroom at night she must first wake her husband because she fears walking down the dark hall alone.

When I heard the story of this young woman, I just sat in stunned silence. How could anyone make sense out of that? She'll feel the effects of it for the rest of her life. Steve's cousin did say that the incident drew her family closer together. It also brought her somewhat closer to God.

But though technically one could point to these things as reasons why God allowed all of this to happen, surely they couldn't be the whole story. She had already been close to God, and they already had a better-than-average family life. Surely God's whole purpose couldn't have been just to move their good family life and Christian life up a few notches. A much milder trial could have done that. What was God thinking? The burden of the questions seemed to outweigh the answers.

If I was to be involved in a ministry to people who suffer, it seemed to me that I should know the solutions to questions like these. But how could I help others understand what I didn't even understand myself?

I will always be grateful for a book which God sent into my life about that time, one which I say without hesitation is among the best I have ever read. In his book *Knowing God,* J. I. Packer included a small chapter called "God's Wisdom and Ours." There he tackles this very problem of our inability to understand the purposes of God behind every event.

> Now the mistake that is commonly made is to . . . suppose . . . that the gift of wisdom consists in an ability to see why God has done what He has done in a particular case, and what He is going to do next.

What do you mean that's a mistake? Isn't wisdom the ability to always figure out the mind of God?

> People feel that if they were really walking closer to God, so that He could impart wisdom to them freely, then . . . they would discern the real purpose of everything that happened to them, and it would be clear to them every moment how God was making all things work together for good. . . . If they end up baffled, they put it down to their own lack of spirituality.

He's sure got my number. Has this guy been reading my mind?

> Such people spend much time . . . wondering why God should have allowed this or that to take place . . . or what they should deduce from it . . . Christians . . . may drive themselves almost crazy with this kind of futile inquiry.

Amen to that! I'm about to go bananas myself. Then you mean that we can't always understand what God is thinking? Wow, I thought. *Then if that isn't wisdom, what is?* The next few pages held some answers that were real life-changers for me, and that got me searching in the Bible for some answers of my own.

I came across the story of Job, the classic example of suffering. If anyone ever needed to understand the "why" behind his condition, it was Job, His family had been killed, his property ruined and stolen, and his body inflicted with boils. Not until the last five chapters of the book does God finally walk onstage to answer the questions and challenges of Job and his friends. And when He does, do you know what reason God gives Job for all the suffering he has experienced? None. Not a word! He doesn't sit Job down and say, "Listen carefully while I give you the inside story on why I've let you go through all of this. You see, My plan is . . . ." In fact, so far is God from answering Job's questions that He says, "Stand up, Job. I've got a few questions to ask *you!*"

For the next four chapters God does nothing but describe in detail the awesome majesty of His own works in nature, and then asks Job if he can match them. The Lord paints vivid word pictures of the creation of the world, the vastness of the stars and space, the might of the ox, the majesty of the horse, the miracle of animal instincts and the way earth provides food for every living thing. "But of course you know all this!" God mocks Job, "For you were born before it was all created, and you are so very experienced!" (Job 38:21, LB).

I could almost feel Job cringing as God spoke to him. (I was cringing myself.) *Why put Job on the spot?* I thought. All those descriptions of God's wisdom and power in nature were certainly interesting. But what did they have to do with Job's trials? Job never claimed he had created the world. He never said he could explain the habits of wild animals. Why was God talking about that? Job hadn't pretended to know all the mysteries of weather cycles and birth and life. All he wanted was for God to help him understand the death of his family, the loss of his property, and the boils all over his body.

I continued reading. More nature scenes. More descriptions of God's greatness. More taunts from God like "Do you know how mountain goats give birth? . . . Can you shout to the clouds and make it rain? . . . Do you realize the extent of the earth? . . . Tell Me about it if you know!"

It still seemed so confusing. But as I came to chapter forty, some light began to dawn. God finally asked Job a question that seemed to focus in on what He had been driving at all along. "Do you still want to argue with the Almighty! Or will you yield? Do you—God's critic—have the answers? . . . Stand up like a man and brace yourself for battle. Let me ask you a question, and give me the answer. Are you going to discredit my justice and condemn me, so that you can say you are right?" (Job 40:1, 7-8, LB).

So that was it! God understood that when Job demanded "Why?" he was really asking God to be accountable to him. It seems so innocent, but in a sense, to insist on such answers from God is to set oneself over God. How absurd! We, like Job, often think God is not treating us fairly. We act as if there were some imaginary court in the sky where God must answer to something called "fairness." But what we forget is that God Himself *is* the court; and He invented fairness. What could we possibly measure His fairness against? What He does is as fair as you can get.[20]

Look at God's awesome wisdom and power demonstrated by His marvelous works of creation. How could such a God be answerable to a puny mortal like Job, who couldn't begin to fathom God's infinite greatness? As God said in Jeremiah 49:19, "Who is like Me, and who will summon Me into court?" It was as if God were saying, "Job, if you can't even understand the way I do things in the natural world, what gives you a right to question Me in the spiritual realm, which is even harder to understand?"

When Job realized this, all he could say was, "I am nothing—how could I ever find the answers? I lay my hand upon my mouth in silence. I have said too much already" (Job 40:4-5, LB).

What made Job feel this way? He got his first glimpse of who God really is. All his life he had worshiped God, but for the first time he saw God as He really is, not just his own limited concept of Him. Job put it like this: "I had heard about you before, but now I have seen you, and I loathe myself and repent in dust and ashes" (Job 42:5, LB).

My thoughts turned away from Job's situation and back to my own. I was grateful for the things I had been able to see from God's point of view. But, like Job, I still had unanswered questions. What about the things God hadn't revealed? How had I handled them?

Immediately I was convicted. The Bible tells us our God is so trustworthy that we are to throw our confidence on Him, not leaning on our own limited understanding (Prov. 3:5). God has already proved how much His love can be trusted by sending Christ to die for us. Wasn't that enough? Not for me. I always wanted to be on the inside looking out—sitting with the Lord up in the control tower instead of down on the confusing ground level. He couldn't be trusted unless I was there to oversee things!

What a low view of my Master and Creator I had held all these years! How could I have dared to assume that almighty God owed me explanations! Did I think that because I had done God the "favor" of becoming a Christian, He must now check things out with me? Was the Lord of the universe under obligation to show me how the trials of every human being fit into the tapestry of life? Had I never read Deuteronomy 29:29: "There are secrets the Lord your God has not revealed to us" (LB)?

What made me think that even if He explained all His ways to me I would be able to understand them? It would be like pouring million-gallon truths into my one-ounce brain. Why, even the great apostle Paul admitted that, though never in despair, he was often perplexed (2 Cor. 4:8). Hadn't God said, "For as the heavens are higher than the earth, so are . . . my thoughts [higher] than your thoughts" (Isa. 55:9)? Didn't one Old Testament author write, "As you do not know the path of the wind, or how the body is formed in a mother's womb, so you cannot understand the work of God, the Maker of all things" (Eccl. 11:5, NIV)? In fact, the whole book of Ecclesiastes was written to convince people like me that only God holds the keys to unlocking the mysteries of life and that He's not loaning them all out! "He has also set eternity in the hearts of men; yet they cannot fathom what God has done from beginning to end" (Eccl. 3:11, NIV).

If God's mind was small enough for me to understand, He wouldn't be God! How wrong I had been.

I thought back to those early days of studying God's Word when the puzzle pieces of my suffering began fitting together. How sweet that first taste of wisdom was. There's nothing like seeing our difficulties from God's perspective. But what a mistake to think that I would ever be able to complete the *whole* puzzle of suffering. For wisdom is more than just seeing our problems through God's eyes—it's also trusting Him even when the pieces don't seem to fit.

WHEN IT ALL FITS TOGETHER

16 Heaven

"Clouds," I mumbled to myself, staring out the window of the plane.

"Hmm?" Sheryl glanced up from her book.

"Those clouds out there," I answered. "Look at them."

Sheryl leaned over my shoulder and stared out at the beautiful expanse of puffy billows. It was close to dusk, and the cloudscape was one of the most gor-

geous we had ever seen—deep purples, light pinks, hazy blues, bright oranges: a celestial mountain range arrayed in panorama against the setting sun.

"What do they remind you of?" I asked.

"Mountains," she said. "Spongy mountains in a million colors."

"I know," I answered, eyes still fixed on the view. "You'd almost believe they'd hold you up if you jumped out onto them."

But they wouldn't. Beautiful as they were, solid as they seemed, they were just fading mists of vapor—wisps of smoke. Here today, gone tomorrow.

I thought about our life here on earth and what the Bible says about it. "What is your life? You are a mist that appears for a little while and then vanishes" (James 4:14). I glanced about the cabin of the plane. Stewardesses serving refreshments. Businessmen with their *Wall Street Journals.* Mothers and babies. Tourists with tennis rackets. Some dozing. Some staring out the window. Flying to sales meetings, vacations, grandchildren.

It doesn't seem like a mist that quickly vanishes, I thought to myself. *We really don't believe it's all going to end, do we? If God hadn't told us differently, we'd all think this parade of life would go on forever.*

But it will end. This life is not forever.

Nor is it the best life that will ever be. The good things here are merely images of the better things we will know in heaven. It's like the artwork I produce. I draw scenes from nature around me, but those drawings are only a feeble, sketchy attempt to mirror what I see. I imitate with a gray pencil what God has painted with an infinite array of colors. My drawings, bounded by the edges of a sketch pad, can never fully portray God's boundless nature above, beneath, and around us. And just as my artwork pleasantly but imperfectly reflects the nature I see, so

this earth that we know is only a preliminary sketch of the glory that will one day be revealed. Reality—the final painting—lies in heaven.

Our problem is—we get too caught up in the "reality" of life.

"A month from now I'll be sipping lemonade on the sands of Florida," dreams the overworked secretary.

"Three more weeks till we're out of here!" thinks the high school senior looking forward to graduation.

"Isn't he the most wonderful person on earth," sighs the engaged young woman.

"If only I get this promotion," plans the rising executive.

But getting what we want is seldom as wonderful as our imagination told us it would be. The long-awaited vacation ends up being too short and too expensive. College assignments make high school homework seem like child's play. The maiden's knight turns out to be an average husband with chinks in his armor. And that promotion at the office brings with it added pressure and headaches. The good things in life rarely turn out to be as satisfying as we expect. And even when they do, they never last long enough.

That's why God tells us in the Bible that we are to set our hearts on heaven (Col. 3:2; 1 Peter 1:13). Life's pleasures were never meant to fill us. They are merely to whet our appetite for what is to come—and to cheer and inspire us as we trek through this earth toward heaven. "Our Father refreshes us on the journey with some pleasant inns, but He will not encourage us to mistake them for home."[21]

The trouble is, we do mistake them for home. It's hard to think about heaven when it seems so far away. Besides, we've got to die in order to get there.

Who wants to think about that! And so God gives us a little help in getting our minds on the hereafter. He does it in a way we usually don't appreciate at first, but later we're grateful for it. Samuel Rutherford described this help in an essay he wrote back in the seventeenth century:

> If God had told me some time ago that he was about to make me as happy as I could be in this world, and then had told me that he should begin by crippling me in arm or limb, and removing me from all my usual sources of enjoyment, I should have thought it a very strange mode of accomplishing his purpose. And yet, how is his wisdom manifest even in this! For if you should see a man shut up in a closed room, idolizing a set of lamps and rejoicing in their light, and you wished to make him truly happy, you would begin by blowing out all his lamps; and then throw open the shutters to let in the light of heaven.[22]

That's just what God did for me when He sent a broken neck my way. He blew out the lamps in my life which lit up the here and now and made it so exciting. The dark despair which followed wasn't much fun. But it sure did make what the Bible says about heaven come alive. One day, when Jesus comes back, God is going to throw open heaven's shutters. And there's not a doubt in my mind that I'll be fantastically more excited and ready for it than if I were on my feet. You see, *suffering gets us ready for heaven*.

How does it get us ready? *It makes us want to go there*. Broken necks, broken arms, broken homes, broken hearts—these things crush our illusions that earth can "keep its promises." When we come to *know* that the hopes we cherished will never come true, that our dead loved one is gone from this life forever, that we will never be as pretty, popular, successful, or famous as we had once imagined, it lifts our sights. It moves our eyes from this world, which God knows could never satisfy us anyway, and sets them on the life to come. Heaven becomes our passion.

When I think of longing for heaven, I think of Rick Spaulding, a 23-year-old paralytic who wrote me shortly after reading my first book. His letters were so full of joy and love for the Lord that they encouraged all of us who read them. I thought I would enjoy meeting him someday; perhaps I could find out more about his injury, and we could share spiritual insights or talk shop about wheelchairs.

On July 4, 1976, I had opportunity to visit Rick. Some friends had taken me to Philadelphia for a few days where I had several speaking engagements. On that bicentennial afternoon we had nothing scheduled. So remembering from Rick's letters that he and his family lived in Valley Forge, not far away, we called and asked if we could come see them. Within minutes we were on our way.

When we arrived at the house, Mrs. Spaulding drew us aside to explain a bit about Rick's condition and prepare us for meeting him.

"Rick was in a fist fight at school when he was fifteen," she described. "He fell and hit his head on the gym floor, which put him in a coma. When he woke up, he was paralyzed."

Well, I thought, *so he's paralyzed. I'm paralyzed.*

But she went on to tell us just *how* paralyzed he was. You see, I can move my shoulders. I can move a little bit of my biceps muscles. I can smile and talk. But Rick couldn't do any of these things. The most he could do was turn his head and blink his eyes—and it had taken him months to learn even that.

"You're going to have to learn to read eyelids," she warned, and in we went.

From the moment we met Rick, we liked him.

There he lay in a reclining chair, unable to chew his food and unable to speak a word. But could those eyes ever talk! As we communicated (for we could not actually converse), I learned to ask the type of question he could most easily answer—questions to which he could blink a "yes" or a "no."

Rick's parents shared with us a method they had discovered which allowed Rick to make full sentences. It was an alphabet chart. Whenever he wanted to spell a word, his mom would watch as he pointed his eyes to either the right or left side of the chart. Then he'd look up, straight ahead, or down to indicate which line he wanted. Finally his mom would read aloud each letter on that line until he blinked. She'd write the appropriate one down, and he'd go on to another.

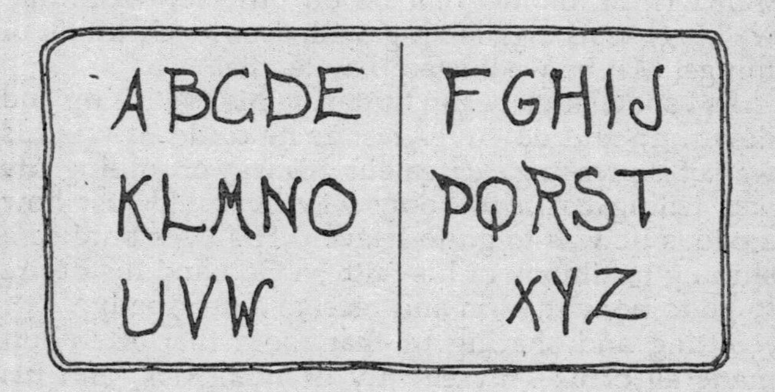

By using the chart to write term papers and by listening to his textbooks on tape, Rick had gone on to finish high school and two years of college. In his college work he received one A, one C, and the rest Bs! (His only C was his first semester of Russian language. He later pulled it up to a B.)

We "talked" about a lot of things that afternoon, but the most exciting time was when we began talking about our mutual faith in the Lord and about heaven.

"Rick," I said, hoping to express for him what he could not, "can you believe how neat it's going to be when we get our new bodies in heaven!"

His eyes lit up.

"I don't know about you," I continued, "but when I was on my feet I never thought much about heaven. I pictured it as a boring place where everyone wore angel costumes, propped their feet up on clouds, and polished gold all day long."

Rick laughed although he couldn't smile (if you can imagine that).

"But since I lost the use of my body, I've learned that one day I'm going to trade it in for a new one.[23] No angel wings! Just hands that work and feet that walk. Think of it. We'll be on our feet—running, walking, working, talking with Jesus—all kinds of things! Maybe we'll even play tennis!

As I spoke Rick began fluttering his eyelids up and down, up and down, as fast as he could. It was his way of expressing excitement, his way of smiling. He was telling us in the only way he could just how anxious he was to go to heaven. His eyes blinked a shining testimony of his faith in God and his desire to go to be with Him and receive a new body.

Sitting and sharing in that room that afternoon made all of us—myself, my friends, Rick, and his family—long for heaven. But since Rick had the most to gain by going there, I think he longed for it most. One month later he got his wish. In August of that same year, Rick went to be with the Lord.

What suffering did for Rick, it can do for all of us—get our hearts on things above, where they belong. But suffering does more than make us want to go to heaven. *It prepares us to meet God when we get there.*

Just think for a moment. Suppose you had never in your life known any physical pain. How could you at all appreciate the scarred hands with which Christ will greet you? What if no one had ever hurt you deeply? How could you adequately express your gratefulness when you approach the throne of the Man of Sorrows who was acquainted with grief (Isa. 53:3)? If you had never been embarrassed, if you had never felt ashamed, you could never begin to know just how much He loved you when He took your shameful sins and made them His.

Don't you see—when we meet Him face to face, our suffering will have given us at least a *tiny* taste of what He went through to purchase our redemption? We will appreciate Him so much more. And our loyalty in those sufferings will give us something to offer Him in return. For what proof could we bring of our love and faithfulness if this life had left us totally unscarred? What shame would we feel if our Christianity had cost us nothing? Suffering prepares us to meet God.

And suffering does one more thing. If in our trials we are faithful, *they win for us rich rewards in heaven.* "For our light and momentary troubles are achieving for us an eternal glory that far outweighs them all" (2 Cor. 4:17). It's not merely that heaven will be a wonderful place *in spite of* all our sufferings while on earth. Actually, it will be that way *because* of them. My wheelchair, unpleasant as it may be, is what God uses to change my attitudes and make me more faithful to Him. The more faithful I am to Him, the more rewards will be stored up for me in heaven. And so our earthly sufferings don't just aid us today; they will serve us in eternity.

Now I don't know exactly what these rewards and treasures will be, but they'll be worth it. Remember back in second grade when one of the kids was the class hero because he had an especially neat yo-yo? To all the other kids, what mattered most in the world was to own the same kind of yo-yo. But when you were in high school, you no longer cared about yo-yos. Then what mattered most was being on the varsity team, or owning a sporty car, or being popular with a certain crowd.

In the same way, when God gives us our perfect hearts, the things that matter so much to us now won't seem important any more. The passion of our hearts will be to honor Him who alone is worthy of praise. In one sense, those who have been faithless in this life, to whom God does not give many rewards, will probably not want them. I believe their purified hearts will gladly admit that they don't deserve them. And those to whom God gives rewards? It seems that all they will want will be to serve God more fully and completely. And He will grant them their wish. They will be privileged to serve Him in special ways—as rulers over His affairs and pillars in His temple (Matt. 25:23; Rev. 3:12).

I said that one day God will give us perfect hearts. To me, that seems the single greatest marvel about heaven. If God were to take us to heaven today without changing us inside, heaven wouldn't be heaven. The purity and holiness there would only repel us and make us feel guilty. And we'd become terribly bored after awhile, just as we do with even the most exciting activities on earth.

The thing that will make heaven heavenly will be the change God will make inside us. Can you imagine what it will be like to never again have the desire to sin? to never again feel guilty? or depressed? or upset? We will know the wonderful harmony of not only being in paradise, but also of having hearts that are able to enjoy it.

* * * *

When I think of heaven, I think of a time when I will be welcomed home. I remember when I was on my feet what a cozy, wonderful feeling it was to come home after hockey practice. How pleasant to hear the familiar clanging of bells against our back door as I swung it open. Inside awaited the sights, sounds, and smells of warmth and love. Mom would greet me with a wide smile as she dished out food into big bowls ready to be set on the table. I'd throw down my sweat suit and hockey stick, bound into the den, and greet daddy. He'd turn from his desk, taking off his glasses, then he'd give me a big "hi" and ask me how practice was.

For Christians, heaven will be like that. We will see old friends and family who have gone on before us. Our kind heavenly Father will greet us with open, loving arms. Jesus, our older brother, will be there to welcome us, too. We won't feel strange or insecure. We will feel like we're home . . . for we *will* be home. Jesus said it was a place prepared for us.

We'll have new bodies and new minds! I myself will be able to run to friends and embrace them for the first time. I will lift my new hands before the hierarchy of heaven—shouting to everyone within earshot, "Worthy is the Lamb who was slain to receive blessing and honor. For He freed my soul from the clutches of sin and death, and now He has freed my body as well!"

The wrongs and injustices of earth will be righted. God will measure out our tears which He has kept in His bottle, and not a single one will go unnoticed. He who holds all reasons in His hand will give us the key that makes sense out of our most senseless sufferings. And that's only the beginning.

> He will wipe every tear from their eyes. There will be no more death or mourning or crying or

> pain, for the old order of things has passed away.

Can't wait?

> He who testifies to these things says, "Yes, I am coming soon."
>
> Amen. Come, Lord Jesus.
> (Revelation 21:4; 22:20-21)

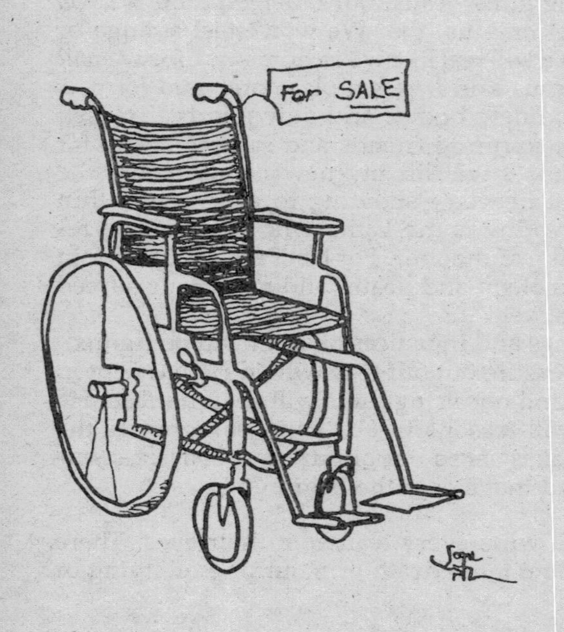

Notes

Page 36

[1]Philippians 1:29.

Page 50

[2]The next two pages are taken from Paul's argument in 2 Corinthians 10-13. Many of the ideas have come from: Frederick D. Bruner, *A Theology of the Holy Spirit* (Grand Rapids: Eerdmans Publishing Co., 1970), pp. 303-315; Walter J. Chantry, *Signs of the Apostles*, rev. (Edinburgh, Scotland: Banner of Truth Trust, 1973), pp. 71-81.

Page 67

[3]C. S. Lewis, *The Problem of Pain* (New York: Macmillan Publishing Co., Inc., 1962), p. 93.

Page 78

[4]Ibid.

[5]John W. Wenham, *The Goodness of God* (Downers Grove: Inver-Varsity Press, 1974), p. 56.

Page 89

[6]Lewis, *Pain*, pp. 43-44.

Page 102

[7]Source for this idea was Edith Schaeffer, *A Way of Seeing* (Old Tappan, N. J.: Fleming H. Revell Co., 1975), p. 64.

Page 110

[8]Romans 12:15.

Page 134

[9]Please don't misunderstand and think that when we call disease a result of sin we mean that every time someone is sick or deformed it is because of some specific sin or sins in his or her life. Jesus' disciples made this mistake once. Upon seeing a man who was blind from birth, they asked Jesus, "'Rabbi, who sinned, this man or his parents, that he was born blind?'" But Jesus corrected their misconception. "'Neither this man nor his parents sinned,' said Jesus, 'but this happened so that the work of God might be displayed in his life'" (John 9:1-3). Then He healed the man. Now Jesus wasn't saying that the man and his parents were totally sinless. He merely meant that the man's blindness was not the result of some direct sin. It was part of the general curse from God that the human race must suffer collectively because of its sin.

Page 135

[10]While the other Gospels use the phrase "the kingdom of God," Matthew alone uses the phrase "the kingdom of heaven." Although many Christians take these to be two different things, it is our belief that the two phrases are interchangeable and refer to the same thing. A quick comparison of parallel passages in Matthew and the other Gospels will bear this out. Compare Matthew 4:17 with Mark

1:15, and Matthew 13:11 with Mark 4:11 and Luke 8:10.

Matthew's Gospel is directed at Jewish readers who hesitated to verbalize the name of God for fear of misusing it and, therefore, often substituted "heaven" or some other word for "God." See, for example, Luke 15:21: "Father, I have sinned against heaven and against you'" (also Matthew 21:25, and Mark 14:61 where "the Blessed" is used to refer to God). Thus, "the kingdom of heaven" is merely the Jewish form of the phrase, "the kingdom of God," the Greek form.

[11]Several other references to the kingdom as partially present now, or as present in some senses now, are: Colossians 1:13; Romans 14:17; 1 Corinthians 4:20; Matthew 13:44-46; Mark 12:34; Matthew 12:28; and Luke 17:20-21.

If this view of the kingdom was interesting or helpful to you and you would like to investigate it further, see: George Ladd, *The Presence of the Future* (Grand Rapids: Eerdmans Publishing Co., 1974), pp. 45-119; *Crucial Questions About the Kingdom of God* (Grand Rapids: Eerdmans Publishing Co., 1974); *The Gospel of the Kingdom* (Grand Rapids: Eerdmans Publishing Co., 1959); Herman Ridderbos, *The Coming of the Kingdom* (Nutley, N. J.: Presbyterian and Reformed Publishing Co., 1975).

Our primary purpose here is not to enter any sort of debate over eschatology (i.e., the doctrine of Christ's second coming). In our presentation of the kingdom of God as partially present and partially future, we are merely trying to say that God has not totally finished everything He is going to do in removing sin and sin's results. (Christians of all eschatological persuasions will agree with this.) Using the concept of the kingdom of God merely seemed to us to be the simplest yet clearest way of doing this.

Page 136

[12]This verse could also be translated "the kingdom of God is within you," but since Jesus was talking to men who didn't believe in Him, some versions prefer the equally acceptable reading "the kingdom of God is among you" or "is in your midst" (NASV).

[13]See Matthew 6:10; 25:31-34; Mark 14:25; Galatians 5:21; 2 Thessalonians 1:5; Revelation 11:15.

Page 141

[14]John 14:30; 12:31; Matthew 28:18; Colossians 2:15; Hebrews 2:14; 1 John 4:4; Daniel 4:35; Isaiah 40:25; John 1:3; Job 1:12; 2:6; Mark 1:24; 5:7; 1:27; Romans 16:20; Revelation 20:1-3, 10.

Page 144

[15]"Thine eyes are too pure to approve evil and Thou canst not look on wickedness with favor" (Hab. 1:13); "For God cannot be tempted by evil, nor does he tempt anyone" (James 1:13). "God is the author of the author of evil, but he cannot be the author of sin itself for sin is the result of a rebellion against God. How can God rebel against himself?" (E. J. Carnell, *An Introduction to Christian Apologetics* [Grand Rapids: Eerdmans Publishing Co., 1948], p. 302).

"All evil is either sin or the punishment for sin" (Carnell, p. 2). God can be said to be the author of the punishment for sin (calamity, hell, etc.), but the Bible will not allow us to call Him the author of sin itself, even though His plan allowed it to come about. Though we can't understand this, still we cannot "draw a straight line" between God and sin.

Page 151

[16]1 Corinthians 9:1-3; 2 Corinthians 2:17; 11:23 ff.

Page 152

[17]In the first five chapters of Acts, only the apostles are mentioned as performing miracles (Acts 2:43; 3:6; 4:33; 5:12; 5:15-16). In Acts 6:6 the apostles laid hands on seven godly men (all non-apostles) and prayed for them. Among these men were Stephen and Philip. Immediately the text records the fact that Stephen did miracles among the people (6:8). After the account of Stephen (6:8-7:60), the text records the fact that Philip worked miracles in Samaria. The clear implication is that they got this ability when the apostles laid hands on them.

It seems also that non-apostles were not able to transfer their miraculous gifts to others without the aid of an apostle. When the apostles heard that the Samaritans had "accepted the Word of God" (8:14), they sent Peter and John to Samaria because "the Holy Spirit had not yet come upon any of them; they had simply been baptized into the name of the Lord Jesus" (8:16). When the apostles laid hands on the Samaritans, they "received the Holy Spirit" (8:17).

Some students feel that the Samaritans were not truly saved until Peter and John came, for how could a person be saved without having the Holy Spirit? It seems more likely to us, however, that "they received the Holy Spirit" means "they received the miraculous gifts of the Spirit." For one thing, 8:14 says that the Samaritans "accepted the Word." For another, in 8:18 Simon the Sorcerer, "*saw* that the Spirit was given at the laying on of the apostles' hands." This implies that the Samaritans received outward, visible signs, not an inward work of grace. It seems, therefore, that as a non-apostle (in the technical sense of the word "apostle"), Philip received miraculous gifts from under the supervision of the apostles. It seems also that those receiving such gifts were not able to confer the power to others without the aid of the apostles *themselves*.

[18]Deuteronomy 29:5. This idea came from *Miraculous Healing* by Henry Frost (soon available from Zondervan).

Page 162

[19]Even the apostle Paul did once! See Acts 16:6-7.

Page 178

[20]It seems to me personally that our failure to have as complete and perfect an understanding of "fairness" as God does stems from two things. First, we just don't have all the facts. Trying to decide if what He does in a given situation is fair or not is like coming into a room halfway through an argument. Not having all the background information, we are in no real position to cast a verdict. And we won't have all the information until Judgment Day, when we'll be able to see things in light of an eternal perspective.

The second reason we don't always view what God does as fair is our own failure to appreciate the seriousness and hideousness of sin. I know that it seldom really strikes me that God owes this utterly rebellious and ungrateful planet absolutely *nothing*. In fact, that is an understatement. Actually, He does owe us something—hell. My father once commented how strange it is that we Christians say we deserve hell, but then complain when we get the slightest taste of it here on earth. If we just for once could have a clear picture of the extent of our own sin, I'm sure we could agree with C. S. Lewis when he says that "the real problem is not why some humble, pious, believing people suffer, but why some do *not*" (Lewis, *Pain*, p. 104).

One objection that is often raised against attributing fairness to God goes as follows: "There are some things God allows in the world that seem so unfair to us (e.g., children dying in war, etc.) that if God were to call them 'fair' we must be using a totally different dictionary than He. If our 'black' is His 'white,' the discussion becomes meaningless." C. S. Lewis answers this objection convincingly (*Pain*, pp. 37-39). If you are wrestling with the whole issue of God's goodness, by all means read this excellent book.

Page 186

[21]Lewis, *Pain*, p. 115.

Page 187

[22]Samuel Rutherford, *Letters of Samuel Rutherford.*

Page 190

[23]1 Corinthians 15:42-44; 2 Corinthians 5:1-2.

Some Books You Might Enjoy

Biographies and Autobiographies

Elliot, Elisabeth. *These Strange Ashes.* New York: Harper and Row, 1975.

If you profited from the chapter "Let God Be God," you will enjoy this book. A main theme underlying it is that God often sends trials we just don't understand, and that He is to be trusted anyway.

Elliot, Elisabeth. *Through Gates of Splendor.* Old Tappan, N.J.: Fleming H. Revell, Co., 1975.

Linke, Maria Zeitner, with Hunt, Ruth. *East Wind.* Grand Rapids, Mich.: Zondervan Publishing House, 1976.

Myra, Harold. *Elsbeth*. Old Tappan, N.J.: Fleming H. Revell, Co., 1976.

Ten Boom, Corrie and Sherrill, John. *The Hiding Place*. Old Tappan, N.J.: Fleming H. Revell, Co., 1975.

Vanauken, Sheldon. *A Severe Mercy*. New York: Harper and Row, 1977.

Dealing With Suffering

Clarkson, Margaret. *Grace Grows Best in Winter.* Grand Rapids, Mich.: Zondervan Publishing House, 1975.

This sister in Christ, who is an inspiration to me each time our paths cross, knows what it is to live in pain. Each chapter is a short devotional in itself, discussing suffering in body, soul, and spirit.

Lloyd-Jones, Martyn. *Spiritual Depression.* Grand Rapids, Mich.: Wm. B. Eerdmans Publishing Company, 1965.

Short sermons on Bible passages that deal with emotional and spiritual suffering. Excellent!

Yancey, Philip. *Where Is God When It Hurts.* Grand Rapids, Mich.: Zondervan Publishing House, 1977.

Although Philip and I take a somewhat different view of God's sovereignty, I thoroughly enjoyed this fascinating, well-written book. It includes such helpful topics as "Why is there pain?" and "How can we cope with it?" The personal stories of others who hurt are especially interesting.

Healing

Frost, Henry. *Miraculous Healing.* Soon available from Zondervan Publishing House.

For anyone who wants to go deeper into the subject, this is the finest little book I know. The language is a bit turn-of-the-century, but not really difficult. Actual case histories make it especially valuable.

How Can a Good God Allow Suffering

Lewis, C.S. *The Problem of Pain.* New York: Macmillan, 1943.

Wenham, John. *The Goodness of God.* Downers Grove, Ill.: Inter-Varsity Press, 1974.

The Nature of God

Packer, J. I. *Knowing God.* Downers Grove, Ill.: Inter-Varsity Press, 1973.

Without a doubt, what helps us most in accepting and dealing with suffering is an adequate view of God—learning who He is and knowing He is in control. Dr. Packer's book helped me so much with this, especially the chapter "These Inward Trials."

You can contact Joni at:

Joni and Friends
P.O. Box 3225
Woodland Hills, CA 91365